V 9

kim.otbc@gmail.com
sidscape4@gmail.com

Prologue

Though they carry the weight of
unrequested burdens, they are not The Other.

They are us, differently accented.

Table of Contents

Section 1.
Introduction

The guiding principle expressed within the text of On the Level is that this work is primarily an educational and informing document, rather than an assessment tool. The fundamental purpose of this work is to educate, clarify, and expand the reader's understanding of the behavioral and cognitive characteristics of the autism spectrum.

With that said we also need to acknowledge that the educational function and the evaluation process cannot be completely insulated from one another, nor should they be. As a matter of good practice they often inform and enhance each other.

An assessment-diagnostic instrument surely requires the supporting armature of definitions and illustrative examples in order to develop a useful – and hopefully accurate – array of assessment modalities. And by way of reciprocity, as the assessment modalities evolve toward greater accuracy and depth, the information that emerges from the application of these methods can be fed back to the researchers and system-builders who in turn can modify and sharpen the definitions, structure and signature characteristics of the area that is being studied.

The development of the material in this work proceeds on the assumption that the people and organizations who are involved with the autism community will be able to expand and deepen their awareness of "the spectrum" by having access to reference and illustrative materials that are a) logically arranged and b) sufficiently comprehensive and specific to promote detailed understanding.

The current edition of the Diagnostic and Statistical Manual, Fifth Edition (DSM-5, 2013) defines the autism spectrum condition in terms of two major criteria, i.e. behavioral-cognitive areas, and three levels of severity. The two major diagnostic criteria are A) the enduring presence of impairments in social communication and social relationships and B) the enduring presence of restrictive, repetitive behaviors and the accompanying enduring presence of restrictive, repetitive cognitive processes.

Each of these two major diagnostic criteria are assigned three levels of severity, presented as Level 1, Level 2, and Level 3. It can be assumed that these numerical Levels correspond to the descriptive terms of Mild, Moderate, and Severe degrees of impairment.

The DSM-5 definition of Autism Spectrum Disorder provides three examples of impairments in the social communication and social interaction diagnostic criterion A, and four examples of impairments in the restricted, repetitive behaviors and cognitive processes of diagnostic criterion B. The text states that the given examples are illustrative, not exhaustive. The DSM-5 criteria for an autism spectrum disorder diagnosis may be viewed on pages 50-51 of the text. The three levels of severity can be seen on page 52.

The paradigm that is presented in this work intends to be balanced, detailed, and extensive. A representation of the autism spectrum that offers a comprehensive view should not be solely limited to a description of those behaviors that are problematic or symptomatic. A fully-functioning model of the autistic spectrum needs to include sections or zones that are free of autistic characteristics. Paradoxically, it is the presence of those "free zones" that confer fidelity on the model. A balanced, fully-ranging system provides, in a clear way, the opportunity for the person to be seen as typical, functioning at normatively expected developmental levels of expression or activity. So, in everyday life we will find individuals who stand "on the spectrum" for some Domains, and yet who are also definitely "<u>off</u> the spectrum" for some other Domains. A valid matrix should allow both possibilities to occur with equal ease.

The DSM-5 has done away with the diagnoses of *Asperger Disorder* and *Pervasive Developmental Disorder Not Otherwise Specified*, both of which were previously closely affiliated with autism spectrum disorders. Neither one of these discarded diagnoses (or categories) may now be validly used for new medical records or billing-for-compensation purposes. Nevertheless, the category of Asperger Disorder continues to carry meaningful communication value and thus continues to be used in the contexts of topical discussion and informal description. Perhaps if the category continues to demonstrate its communication utility over time it might be "rehabilitated" and returned to future editions of the DSM.

Section 2.
Definitions.

There are a small number of basic concepts that appear throughout this work. In order to establish the effectively shared meaning of these concepts, as they are used within the context of this text, they are presented and defined in the following section.

Domain: A Domain is a general area of behavioral functioning, ability, or observed cognitive style. *On The Level* examines twelve different Domains. Some examples include Social Relationships, Personal Management, Types of Interests, and Pragmatic Language. Synonyms for Domain Are *Area* and *Sector*.

Matrix: The matrix is the grid formed by the intersection of the Domains as one variable, and the seven Levels of severity as the other variable.

Region: The region is the combination of all those Domains that are seen to be operating in the range of autism characteristics. Thus, we can speak of the autism region and likewise refer to the autism-free region.

Participant: There are a variety of different possible category-identifiers that refer to the people whose behavioral characteristics are described in the seven Levels. These category-identifiers include identity-descriptive terms such as child, youth, individual, person, student, patient, resident, actor, client and subject. Any of these role-descriptors can be a good fit for some specific contexts. However, an identity-descriptor that is appropriate across a wide range of situations, and which can easily express both typical development as well as developmental disturbance is preferred. For that solution we select the term **participant.** When used in this way, the word refers to someone who is the recipient of observation, description, definition, intervention or support services. The participant can be either actively involved in the events or passively compliant. Each Level of severity will be paired with the name of an illustrative fictitious participant. The entire Domain is presented as the combined narratives of seven individual (fictional) participants. The basic principles and examples contained in those narratives are intended to be relevant for <u>any</u> participant who can be included in those Domains and Levels.

The Domains

A person's skills are a set of tools he or she uses in a variety of contexts. A domain is a particular skill. We have identified **twelve Domains** typically discussed when assessing an individual's "toolbox" of skills. A domain must represent a unique and observable skill or attribute that a person uses. The degrees of skill exhibited are described in the Levels section. But first, the twelve domains, which are listed below.

Domain 1. Social Relationships (SR). This domain covers how the child interacts with others, as well as how important other people are to him.

Domain 2. Language Expression, Expressive Language (ExL). This domain examines the inventory of tools available to the child to communicate her thoughts and needs with others. In Expressive Language, the child's deficits in back-and-forth conversation are mainly a result of an under-developed ability to produce words, phrases and sentences.

Domain 3. Types of Interests (Int). This domain covers the child's interests and activities, their scope, and the extent to which he invites others to participate with him.

Domain 4. Personal Management & Self-Direction (PM). This domain covers the child's abilities to plan, manage, and organize her activities and schedule. It also discusses

"Executive Functions" of prioritizing, initiating, reviewing, obtaining an overview, and screening-out various activities and events.

Domain 5. Language Understanding, Receptive Language (RL). This covers how the child's understanding of words, sentences, phrases, and figures of speech (idioms and proverbs) have developed.

Domain 6. Social Use Language, Pragmatic Language (PL). Pragmatic Language describes the <u>style</u> of language and is related to the child's ability and interest in participating in a balanced, back-and-forth conversation. This domain covers the ways in which the child uses speech and language in conversations and social interactions. It also includes the ways in which the child changes her tone, rate of speech, and voice emphasis in her spoken language.

Domain 7. Body Language. Nonverbal Communication (NC). This domain covers how well the child uses and understands non-verbal communication, communication based on body language, gestures, facial expressions, and eye contact.

Domain 8. Flexibility & Transitions (F/Tn). This domain covers the child's interest in new experiences – whether the child prefers a wide range of activities, or a constant routine. This domain also covers how comfortably the child can transition from one activity to another.

Domain 9. Repeating Body Movements. Movement Stereotypes (MSt). This domain covers how often the child engages in unusual, repeating body movements.

Domain 10. Creative Imagination (CI). This domain covers the child's use of imagination in her daily activities. It also covers the child's preference for an object's real physical properties, rather than the abstract ideas they represent.

Domain 11. Imitation & Empathy (IE). This domain covers the child's ability to understand someone else's feelings, intentions, and experiences, as well as his ability to imitate the behavior of others.

Domain 12. Unusual Sensory Events (USE). This domain covers extreme reactions to sensory input. These may include sounds, discomfort with being touched, fascination with different textures, extreme sensitivity to smells and aromas, unusual reactions to changing patterns of light and flickering light, fascination with the feeling of flowing water, unusual reactions to discomfort or pain, and others.

The Levels

In the context of these discussions the word Level refers to *a conceptual platform that represents a specific band of severity of the Domain (or area) that is being examined.* The model that is represented in this work assigns **seven Levels** of severity to each of the Domains. The Levels and their associated band of severity are presented below.

Level 1.0 Typical Development for Age (Neurotypical). No significant or distinctive autism traits have been observed. This zone of the autism spectrum does not show any prominent autism-related deficits or excesses. However, Domain functioning at Level 1.0 does not exclude the possibility of the presence of other mental health issues.

Level 2.0 Minimum/Trace Slight traces of autism spectrum characteristics are seen. The observed behaviors and mental characteristics can be thought of as inconveniences or slight departures from normatively-prevalent behavior and cognition. At this Level the traits are not usually considered to be substantially handicapping. This zone of the autism spectrum occupies the space between Typical functioning on one hand, and the appearance of c clearly identifiable autistic characteristics on the other.

Level 3.0 Borderline Autism spectrum traits that interfere with the person's functioning in several different areas are seen. Behavioral and educational interventions in these areas (e.g., interpersonally sensitive use of language, social skills, personal organization, etc) can be useful. However, it is important to understand that on balance the person remains largely competent and functional. People who were at this Level were previously viewed as being candidates for inclusion in the category of Asperger Disorder. A person who is at the Borderline Level can be described as *selectively challenged.*

Level 4.0 Mild At this Level clear and distinctive traits of autism that are significantly handicapping are seen in all or mostly all areas of behavior, thinking, and social-educational functioning. While the autism-spectrum behaviors and traits are present and challenging, the individual still retains the capacity for meaningful participation in many of the social, educational, and vocational activities of daily life. The milder zones of this Level are sometimes designated as "high-functioning autism". A wide range of interventions and supports are needed.

Level 5.0 Moderate Clear and distinctive traits of autism which express definite impairment and that are significantly handicapping are seen in all or nearly all areas of behavior, thinking, and social-educational functioning. These behavioral and mental characteristics have a marked impact on the person's environment, including the physical aspects of their residence, the quality of their personal relationships, the demands placed on caregivers, and the teaching skills of educators. Extensive interventions and supports are required.

Level 6.0 Severe All of the areas of daily living activities are seriously impaired, and extensive interventions, supports, and specialized programming are required. The individual's behavioral and mental characteristics have a large and nearly constant stressful impact on their environment.

These impacts include concern for physical security at home, high levels of stressful demands on caregivers, and requirements for detailed instructions for nearly all of the array of independent living skills. Specialized education programs are appropriate.

Level 7.0 Very Severe All of the areas of behavior, use of language, activities of daily living, social relationships, education and vocational placement are very seriously impaired. Extensive interventions, supports and specialized programming are required. These include condition-relevant education, behavioral interventions, family support and respite, supported living arrangements when needed, and specialized vocational or day-activity programs for age-suitable individuals. Ongoing close supervision is recommended. The individual's behavioral and mental characteristics can – and usually do – have a quite large and nearly constant impact on their environment and the people within it. Their needs for remediation are deep and extensive.

Section 3.
Explanatory Notes.

All of the twelve Domains are constructed with seven Levels of severity, and each one of the Levels is linked to the name of a fictitious participant. These linkages between the fictitious name of the participant and the Level are consistent across all twelve Domains. Marcus is always at Level 1.0, Juan is always at Level 3.0, and so forth. This consistency of presentation is used in order to promote ease of discussion about the Levels among the readers of *On The Level*. A second reason for this arrangement is the assumption that the consistency of linkage helps the reader to learn about the features of the various Levels more efficiently.

With that said we wish to emphasize that in actual practice, in "real life", a participant can behave, function, and think at more than one Level. A person's Level of functioning is **not frozen** at a single point. Most participants will typically show variability in their profile, with elevations and dips. Moreover, a participant's profile **can change** over time, given training, education, behavioral intervention and the gains that can come with maturity.

Section 4 of *On The Level* text places the Domain at the top of the page as the <u>main topic</u>. The seven Levels of severity are placed sequentially below the description or the name of the Domain. This arrangement allows the reader to focus on the behavioral-cognitive aspects of a specific Level, as well as the nuanced differences among those seven Levels. For the reader this arrangement places the emphasis on <u>understanding one Domain at a time.</u> This is the **Standard Orientation** of the matrix. The twelve Domains are placed horizontally, and the seven Levels are placed vertically.

Section 5 structures the information of *On The Level* in a different way. The Level and its accompanying definition of severity becomes the main topic placed at the top of the page – or the top of the section. The twelve Domains of the autism spectrum are placed in serial order below the definition (or name) of the Level. The name of each of the Domains is linked to the description of the behavioral-cognitive features of the Level that is the main topic. This is the rotated matrix orientation. The seven Levels are placed horizontally, and the twelve Domains are placed vertically.

The re-arrangement of the descriptive matrix that is presented in Section 5 informs two outcomes. First, when Sections 4 and 5 are considered together they provide an exceptionally complete, nuanced and detailed reference text about the behavioral-cognitive-interactive aspects of the autism spectrum. Second, and perhaps of larger consequence, the matrix that is presented in Section 5 allows the reader to review and understand several Domains concurrently. This aspect of Section 5 can be quite helpful when the reader wishes to compare, as an example, the Level 3.0 Borderline features of Social Relationships with the corresponding Level 3.0 Borderline features of Types of Interests, and then proceed on to Level 3.0 Borderline of the Personal Management & Self-Direction Domain.

In summary, Sections 4 and 5 provide a complimentary perspective, displaying the same descriptions in different formats for an enhanced understanding of the remarkably diverse range of characteristics that is seen across the very wide and seriously deep autism spectrum.

Section 4.
The Domains &
Their Seven Levels of Descriptors, Standard Orientation.

Each of the Twelve Domains are presented as the main topics; levels are arranged in the usual numerical sequence. Each of the Twelve Domains is described and illustrated by the characteristics that are contained in the accompanying Seven Levels.

Domain 1. Social Relationships

This Domain addresses the various ways in which the participants interact with other people, as well as the extent to which other people are important to them.

Level 1.0 Typical Development

Participant: Marcus. The participant's social relationships, friendships and interactions are typical for someone of his age. He looks for friendships and is usually successful in finding them. Alternately, if he is not actively seeking relationships then he is open to developing new ones. Marcus places a high value on being understood and accepted by other people.

Marcus joins in and participates in various group activities. When participating in these activities he understands both the obvious spelled-out rules and the unstated background rules. These two areas of rules can be described as the explicit rules for the activity, and the rules for behaving in the context in which the activity takes place.

The participants at this Level are emotionally connected to some or all of the members of their family, and they very much value their place in the family network.

Level 2.0 Minimum/Trace

Participant: Carmen. The participant Carmen is interested in meeting other people and developing friendships. While often successful, her approach to social interactions is somewhat uncertain and awkward. Carmen is sometimes described as being "slightly out of synch" or "shy".

Carmen has some difficulty understanding some of the more subtle points of social interaction. The problem areas may include her difficulty with understanding the implications of some facial expressions and also the speaker's tone of voice.

Participants at this Level are emotionally connected to other family members and demonstrate, through their behavior and expressions that they value their place within the family. The families usually adjust to these persons' personal style, and when needed compensate for their areas of need. This is usually accomplished without special counseling or professional advice.

Level 3.0 Borderline

Participant: Juan. A participant at this Level would like to have more friends but usually just doesn't seem to know how to do it. Juan usually gets along reasonably well with people who are younger or older than he is, but not so well with his peers. People who are much older or younger than Juan are likely to be more accepting and less critical than people of the same age group. Juan is more likely to develop good friendships when the friends are especially accepting and flexible.

The participant often behaves and speaks in ways that are more formal and stodgy than is usual for people of his age. This speaking style becomes an issue for starting and keeping friendships. Juan is less skillful with the background unstated rules (conventions) of play, games, and social interaction than most people in his age group. Because of this relative shortage of social skills he is frequently not selected for friendships by his peers and unfortunately may indeed be teased or avoided by them.

This degree of rejection by peers can lead to considerable sadness – or even anger, - especially when the socio-cultural context is adolescence, a time when peer relationships take on great importance. These participants get along pretty well with other family members, but not so well with people who are outside the family circle.

Level 4.0 Mild

Participant: Raven. This participant has a definite preference for activities that do not involve interaction with other people. She has very few, if any friends outside of the family, and she is usually not bothered by this situation. When Raven is away from her immediate family she prefers that social interactions be very brief and very limited.

Raven was not a "cuddly" baby or toddler , and did not snuggle. She usually had very little interest in being touched, and she rarely gazed directly into the eyes of nearby people.

Raven will begin an interaction with a family member when she needs something specific, such as food, beverage, access to video games, DVD's, music, computers, or a favorite object. Otherwise she prefers to be left alone.

The participants who are at this Level care about and are emotionally connected to their parents and siblings, and clearly recognize that their parents are important for their well-being and comfort, and further that the parents are the providers of shelter, comfort, guidance, food, and protection.

However, the ways in which Raven expresses those feelings of caring and connection are much more subtle and restrained than those of typical children. For example, she might twirl the parent's hair around her fingers in a matter-of-fact way, or place herself near the parent's lap and accept hugs and expressions of affection without returning the feeling or gesture.

Level 5.0 Moderate

Participant: Dustin. This participant is very selective and sparing about interactions with people. It is not unusual for him to reject or ignore another person's efforts to interact or communicate with him. He can become exhausted or upset when urged to interact with other people. If the request for interaction is too intense or stressful he may become upset, agitated or otherwise misbehave in order to avoid the interaction.

The participant has little or no flexibility regarding the norms of appropriate behavior, which he has learned with considerable effort. Dustin consistently applies these rules or guidelines to specific situations, and continues to apply them even if the context or circumstances change.

He may cooperate briefly when another person makes a request about completing a chore or a school assignment. Then, when left to his own preferences he returns to solitary activity. In the classroom his reaction to the teacher's instructions can be very limited. Dustin often does not acknowledge the presence of other people, and in fact can behave as if they are not there. For example, he might ignore a request to pass a dish at dinner.

As with Level 4.0 these participants were not "cuddly" babies and did not snuggle. They prefer not to be touched, and resist gazing into the eyes of other people.

Dustin and others at this Level rarely show affection openly. They usually do not spontaneously offer hugs, kisses, or gestures of warmth. However, being at home in the presence of their family promote a sense of safety and relative calm. The participants are much more likely to cooperate with members of the family than with newly-introduced people. because family members have the advantage of being familiar, known and therefore trusted.

Level 6.0 Severe

Participant: Susana. The participant does not seek out friends and very rarely reacts or replies to gestures of friendship. Almost all offers of social interactions are rejected.

With steady consistent training at school she can be taught to cooperate with basic activities such as following a group leader to a specific location like a dining area, classroom, recreation area or bus stop.

Susana generally does not show a reaction when a caregiver enters or leaves a room. Her observed behavior appears unattached and unconnected. The participants at this Level may allow a few family members to manage their care.

Level 7.0 Very Severe

Participant: Scott. He completely rejects and avoids all back-and-forth social interaction.

Scott has no interest at all in friendships, social relations, conversations, or pleasantly shared activities (table-top games, card-playing, tossing a ball back-and-forth, dancing). If left to his own preferences all of his activities would be solitary.

Scott is not attached to any caregivers or other family members. He reacts to family members in the same way that he reacts to strangers. Scott and other participants at this Level appear to be stuck in their own world.

Domain 2. Language Expression

This Domain examines the supply (inventory) of speaking-skills that are available to the participants for the purpose of communicating their thoughts and needs to other people. The proficiency described in each of the seven Levels address the participant's relative ability to produce words, phrases, and sentences.

Level 1.0 Typical Development

Participant: Marcus. The participant's language expression abilities are "on track". He is able to speak as many words and word-combinations as most other people in his age group. His use of spoken language is nicely balanced with his ability to understand the statements made by other people. Both of these skills are at an expected level of achievement for Marcus' age-peers.

By the time Marcus was four years old he could say his name and age, develop friendships, sing songs and recite nursey rhymes. Participants who are at least six years old can tell stories, discuss events, and talk about their plans for some future activities such as a birthday party, vacation, camping trip, visit to a theme park, or visit to another family. Marcus is able to speak about these plans in ways that are more detailed and elaborate than just a simple statement of one or two facts.

Level 2.0 Minimum/Trace

Participant: Carmen. The development of language expression abilities in this participant is slightly behind those of other children who are in the same age group.

Her ability to speak words, phrases, and complex sentences are somewhat less skilled or a bit more uncertain than other children in her age-cohort. When the participant was a young child she did not yet master standard English, and because of that could creatively produce phrases and descriptions such as "My shirt is outside out" or "The shoe is upside up".

Despite these small delays in the development of language proficiency this participant maintained an active interest in communicating with other people. Her purposeful use of language is a pathway to maintaining contact with other people, and thus supporting the social-interactive relationship. Even though some of her statements were imperfectly formed, they were nonetheless understood and accepted by the listeners of the conversation.

Level 3.0 Borderline

Participant: Juan. The participant's abilities with language expression can span a wide range, from slightly below average too much below average. Juan's main challenge is in the ways in which he can use language as a method for carrying on a back-and-forth dialogue. For this Level the essential question is that of <u>reciprocity.</u> Can those who are speakers change roles and become listeners? Participants who are at Level 3.0 have more-than-average difficulty with the process of reciprocity. They are more likely to prefer the speakers' role than the listeners' role.

Juan has a style of speaking that is more formal and measured than is usual for young people. For that reason he and other Level 3.0 participants are sometimes described as "Little Professors". (This feature is covered more fully in Domain 4).

Level 4.0 Mild

Participant: Raven. The participant showed a significant delay in the development of speech and language. Either she did not speak in sentences by the time she was three years old, or she was developing language in a normal way and then lost some or all of that skill. A hearing loss may have been suspected.

The participant has definite problems with engaging in a back-and-forth conversation as a result of those difficulties with spoken language. While her ability to engage in conversation is greatly reduced (when compared to Typical development), it is not completely absent. Raven can and does produce meaningful conversations. However, her sentences tend to be brief and limited.

The participants at this Level may show as many as 4 of the following 6 language-and-communication issues:

1. Sometimes replaces the word "I" with the word "he" "she" or "you."

2. Invents their own words. A flashlight might be called a "lightstick" while roller skates could be named "roll shoe".
3. Produce a variety of sounds that are not standard words. Speaks in jargon.
4. Echo or "parrot" words and phrases. This activity is named *echolalia*.
5. Sentences are spoken in a flat tone, or with an unusual rhythm.
6. They prefer to not initiate (start) a conversation with another person.

Level 5.0 Moderate

Participant: Dustin. The production of spoken language is very difficult for Dustin. When sentences are spoken the statements tend to be no longer than three or four words. Dustin can become fascinated with a specific topic or subject, and repeat brief phrases or questions many times. However, the brief phrases or questions are spoken as a matter of intense personal fascination, rather than as a mode of communication. Dustin and other participants whose expressive language skills are at Level 5.0 can also show any of the 6 spoken language variations that are specified (above) in Level 4.0 However, overall speech production is more limited than is seen in Level 4.0.

Dustin may feel more comfortable communicating ideas and requests through the use of various assisted communication devices. These devices include write-boards, picture selection, laptop computers, and electronic digital tablets. For some ASD people the use of American Sign Language is a helpful alternative to communicating by voicing. Elementary skills with American Sign Language can be exercised by children as young as five years of age.

Level 6.0 Severe

Participant: Susana. If spoken language emerged at all after the age of 3, it was extremely limited and incomplete. The number of words that the participant uses are very considerably below average.

If the participant uses spoken language at all it is not for the purpose of promoting social contact or friendly personal interaction. Rather, the small amount of language is used to request valued materials or conditions, such as food, beverages, access to videos, computer games, music, etc. In the absence of spoken language Susana might use gestures and hands-on guidance to obtain those needed materials.

Susana may reply very briefly to a question or statement, but show no interest in extending the exchange into a back-and-forth conversation. She does not look directly at the speaker.

Susana and other participants at her Level can show 3 or 4 of the following speaking and communication issues:

1. Voicing very short sentences, they ask questions repeatedly about a particular topic, but rarely or never show satisfaction with an answer.

2. They echo or "parrot" words and phrases heard either recently or at a much earlier time.
3. They repeat random, non-standard sounds and noises (jargon or babbling).
4. They repeat original, self-created words and phrases. This is done over and over, with no apparent interest in the reactions or attentiveness of other people to the statements

The participants may ignore statements or questions so completely that they appear to not hear at all.

Level 7.0 Very Severe

Participant: Scott. At this Level the language expression skills are extremely below average. Scott and other participants at this Level rarely or never express standard spoken language. If the participant uses language at all it is limited to no more than 4 or 5 words or short phrases per day. These sparse expressions are most likely used to communicate wants, needs, or feelings of discomfort. Scott is likely to use gestures or hands-on guidance to obtain some desired object. Words and sentences are not used for the purpose of engaging in social interaction. .

Scott's inventory of language is not sufficiently well developed to support the kind of repeated questioning or statements about some topic that are seen in Level 5.0 Scott may respond to a statement or question with a movement or an action, but almost never replies with a spoken statement.

Domain 3. Types of Interests

This Domain covers the participant's interests and chosen activities, the scope of these interests, and the extent to which the participant invites other people to participate in these interests and activities.

Level 1.0 Typical Development

Participant: Marcus. The participant developed his skills and learned about his surroundings by sampling a wide variety of activities and experiences. He welcomes the opportunity to explore aspects of his environment.

He likes to share his interests and activities with other people. Importantly, other people serve as an audience that offers encouragement, approval, and guidance for improvement. The adults of the community also set boundaries and procedures that promote safety.

Marcus enjoys learning about a wide variety of topics, and experiences satisfaction and pride from increasing his inventory of knowledge and from recognizing the improvements in his range of useful skills.

Level 2.0 Minimum/Trace

Participant: Carmen. The participant at this Level shows a slight preference for engaging in an individual activity, rather than reaching out for interaction with another person or seeking the attention of an audience. These participants are somewhat less interested than the Typical person in sampling a wide variety of activities and experiences. Some thoughtful planning and well-placed encouragement by her family and teachers can be beneficial in moving the participants at this Level to more skills and wider horizons.

The participant is not very flexible in her attitudes or opinions. She is reluctant to alter an opinion even when given relevant new information. These participants can even be described as "stubborn". By the time this participant is 5 years old she has developed some preferred activities and perhaps a favorite object.

Level 3.0 Borderline

Participant: Juan. By the time Juan is 6 or 7 years old he has developed particularly strong interests, even expertise, in one or two specific subject areas. Some illustrative examples are shipwrecks, reptiles, sports statistics, vocabulary definitions, transportation routes, the pattern of days-of-the-week on a calendar, and detailed computer and electronic equipment operations. The participant may also be very interested in taking objects apart, and most of the time he puts them back together.

The young participant usually takes the initiative in the process of collecting information about the preferred subjects. Adults are useful as sources of information and materials when the young participant is unable to obtain them on his own. The participants at this Level place a great deal of importance on their favorite activities and interests. Participants like Juan are able to focus on these topics for longer spans of time than the typical person. As a result of this heightened capacity for concentration they are able to learn some materials in greater depth and detail than most people usually achieve.

Juan does feel the need to check in, from time to time, with friends and family to share what he is doing, and to maintain his existing social contacts. However, the participant has less need for the attention of an audience than typical participants do, and he often selects activities that do not involve other people.

The Participants at this Level can do well with activities such as swimming, bicycle riding, running, bowling, archery, golf, skating, and tennis. Serious participation in team sports like basketball, baseball, football, soccer, and hockey would be quite unusual.

Level 4.0 Mild

Participant: Raven. The participant has little interest in sampling and learning from a wide variety of experiences.

When the participant becomes involved in a subject or activity, she is focused mostly on the way the activity feels, rather than on how the audience will react to what she is doing. The participant might become very interested in a specific object and then take it apart. However, she has little interest in putting it back together.

Raven shows an on-and-off pattern of attention to what is going on around her. She can be aware of and involved with the surrounding activities for a short span of time. When that span is over she returns to her unshared thoughts, repeating movements, or fascination with some sensory stimulation such as a pattern of lights, the sound of her own voice, or the texture of her clothing.

The participant rarely seeks praise or approval for her accomplishments from those around her. It is also very unusual for her to actively share her activities and interests with other people. Despite this apparent indifference, the participants at this Level can be comforted and reassured by the praise and approval they receive from caregivers, teachers, and mentors.

When praise and approval are offered they can help the participant behave in a calm and constructive way. The participant's difficulties with anticipating or recognizing the consequences of an unsafe activity set boundaries on what she is able to do. The kinds of recreational and sports activities in which Raven can safely participate need to be arranged, organized, and supervised by responsible adults more closely and for a longer span of time than is done for the typical person.

Some participants like Raven express an interest in developing skill in playing a musical instrument. The instrument can be played either in a solo performance, or in association with one or more other musicians. Playing a musical instrument offers a range of choices about the degree of relational directness in which the musician wishes to engage.

Level 5.0 Moderate

Participant: Dustin. The participant has almost no interest in exploring the broad range of activities that most people enjoy. All, or almost all of the participant's interests are concentrated on very specific activities, or on objects that they can touch, move, arrange or otherwise directly experience. Most of these activities can be done in a few steps, usually no more than two or three.

A brief inventory of appropriate recreational activities for participants at this Level may include recreational walking or swimming (with careful supervision), listening to music, viewing a dramatic video, striking a ball with a bat (as in T ball), and finger-painting. Very few of the participant's activities are shared with another person. Dustin may accept another person's participation in the activities, but usually does not request it.

The participant usually has little concern for the presence or reactions of an audience, whether that audience is large or small.

The participants may, from time to time, briefly inspect their surroundings, usually to assure themselves that all is well, and that no sudden changes have been introduced to their routine or living-space.

Level 6.0 Severe

Participant: Susana. The participant has a strong preference for activities that are solitary and focused on objects, whenever she has the opportunity to do so. Susana has little or no interest in the reactions of an audience. The participant does not play games that involve two or more people, and has hardly any understanding or interest in the rules that describe those games.

The participants have little or no interest in activities or topics in which knowledge and useful skill can be increased steadily over a long span of time. The interests of participants at this Level are focused on repeated body movements, sensory stimulation such as a pattern of lights, the sound of their voice, the texture of their clothing, or a limited number of repeated activities.

Level 7.0 Very Severe

Participant: Scott. The participant's behavior is so self-isolating that it is extremely difficult to understand what his interests are, other than repeated body movements or sensory stimulation, as with patterns of lights, the sounds of his voice, or the texture of his clothing.

He will typically focus his attention on a narrow segment of a larger event, such as throwing a ball rather than playing a game of baseball, or moving a single checker on a board instead of playing a full game of checkers.

The participants at this Level have no interest in responding to an audience, and are unconcerned about the ways in which an audience might react to them.

Domain 4. Personal Management & Self-Direction

This Domain addresses the participants' ability to manage, arrange, and effectively follow-through with their activities and schedules. It also discusses the personal management and self-direction skills of setting priorities, starting-and-stopping activities, reviewing and evaluating, and screening out potentially distracting information.

Level 1.0 Typical Development

Participant: Marcus. The participant is able to design, arrange, and manage his activities and materials as effectively as others in his age group. He is able to show a reasonable amount of emotional self-restraint when facing some challenges.

The participant is an effective self-starter and is not overwhelmed at the prospect of starting a project or engaging a series of responsibilities. He can smoothly transition to another activity when the job is completed or the time is up.

The participant is able to stay focused on the job at hand, and disregard or screen out irrelevant, potentially distracting events. The participant has learned how to review, track, and evaluate his work or activities as he goes along. With that awareness in place he is able to effectively self-correct or adjust his efforts in a timely way.

Level 2.0 Minimum/Trace

Participant: Carmen. The participant's goal-setting, activity-planning personal management skills are slightly less well developed than most people in her age group. There can be a lot of variability in the strengths and skill development that co-exist within her collection of personal management and self-direction abilities.

Carmen may need some reminders, suggestions, and short demonstrations in order to keep her schoolwork, clothing, and personal possessions in reasonably good order. While she might be quite good at remembering an array of new information, she might be less effective at deciding which of her activities needed the most effort and attention (setting priorities).

Although the participant's ability to review, evaluate, and self-correct are not so well developed as others in her age-groups, she is open to suggestions and guidance from her family, teachers, and mentors. As a result of that openness to guidance she is generally successful in completing her schoolwork, home chores, vocational assignments and recreational activities.

Level 3.0 Borderline

Participant: Juan. The clash between the participant's personal management and self-direction abilities on one hand, and the presence of disrupting characteristics on the other begin to be seen at this Level.

The dominating aspect of the participant's personal management/self-direction capability is that of selectivity. He seems very skilled at some self-management strategies, and quite unskilled at others.

Some portions of Juan's goal-setting and activity-management skills can be more highly developed than those of the typical participant. He often has the ability to choose a topic of interest and then achieve an unusually high level of skill and competence in that topic.

The participant can very effectively filter-out or disregard competing or distracting background events. However, this heightened ability to focus his attention comes with some costs, such as a reduced ability to smoothly switch from one activity to another. He has a tendency to "stay on track", even when a change would be better for the immediate situation.

The participant's approach to the arrangement of materials, personal possessions, and equipment for projects are likewise very selective. Those materials that fit into his areas of interest are quite well organized. Materials and objects that are outside the scope of his serious interests are often a jumble of disorganization.

The combination of high levels of competence, along with the participant's tendency to ignore or disregard surrounding events lead to the stylistic label of "A young absent-minded professor".

The participants at this Level bring a lot of skill and enthusiasm to their areas of interest, but they often have difficulty with generating an overview, with seeing and understanding "the big picture".

Level 4.0 Mild

Participant: Raven. The clash between the personal management/self-direction resources *versus* the participant's disruptive developmental features increase in intensity at this Level. Raven's difficulty with imagination, combined with a limited tolerance for change have the effect of shrinking her ability to generate and develop an adequate inventory of problem-solving strategies. It is very difficult for her to identify useful alternatives when she has considerable difficulty generating or welcoming new possibilities.

The participant does have a strong interest in arranging objects and activities, as seen in her tendency to arrange personal objects into a specific pattern, as well as a clearly expressed preference for very predictable schedules. (The preference may be expressed behaviorally rather than vocally.)

However, problems develop when objects and materials need to be reorganized in new and creative ways.

The participant is not able to effectively rearrange her possessions, schedules, or activities on a regular basis, without outside help. Her considerable preference for predictable, consistent routines do not fit in very well with the requirements of the personal management/self-direction operations of flexible attention, and the ability to review a variety of alternatives.

It is very difficult for Raven to see "the big picture", the overview. Her natural way of operating is to focus on objects, events, or activities that are specific, real, touchable, and capable of being directly experienced. Moving to an abstract overview is both difficult and unlikely.

Raven and her same-Level peers are able to cooperate in developing the plans or series of steps for managing their work, but are unable to independently create multi-step agendas.

Level 5.0 Moderate

Participant: Dustin. The developmental features that are disruptive have overcome this participant's personal management/self-direction functions, such as his ability to ignore distractions and screen out unimportant background events.

The participant's screening-out function has grown out of proportion, throwing his personal management abilities out of balance. The screening-out function has overwhelmed the other abilities, pushing them aside. As a result Dustin has great difficulty in adjusting or regulating his actions and thinking.

Most of Dustin's attention is focused on some preferred object, movement, pattern of lights or sounds, repeating phrases or behavioral ritual. He usually ignores some useful choices that would allow him to deal with his surroundings more effectively, and thus increase his well-being.

At this Level of behavior (Level 5.0) Dustin is typically not resourceful or flexible enough to generate a "to-do" list of varied activities without significant input and guidance from other people, nor would he effectively accomplish the tasks on that list without specific assistance and guidance from those mentors.

Level 6.0 Severe

Participant: Susana. The extent of the participant's developmental difficulties have thrown her personal management and self-direction functions even further out of balance. As a result almost all of the essential personal management operations need to be put in place by a resource person. The participant is then given the responsibility of carrying out the plans and accomplishing the goals. The process involves ongoing corrections and suggestions for improvements.

Susana and her same-Level peers can still be active participants in the process of developing plans for the daily routine and school activities, in the sense that they are capable of offering some form of approval or disapproval about aspects of the plan. Their feedback is more likely expressed through behavior than through words.

Susana shows the characteristic of a very limiting "tunnel vision". She prefer to focus all, or almost all of her attention on some favorite objects, repeating movements, pattern of light, pattern of sound, repeated phrases or behavioral rituals. The ability to review, track, evaluate, and self-correct her behavior is just about absent.

Level 7.0 Very Severe

Participant: Scott. At this Level the participant does not have the personal management functions that are needed to structure, define, and coordinate his daily activities.

Scott definitely requires the input of another person to provide structuring, guidance, oversight and corrective interventions.

Given careful, skilled and ongoing teaching the participant and his same-Level peers can learn to use a variety of cues and prompts (such as signs, icons, charts, simple pictures, etc.) to travel through the day's schedule of activities. The overall framework of that schedule needs to be designed, adjusted, and sustained by someone else.

In the absence of these structures and supports the participant would slide into a state of self-preoccupation and disorganization.

Domain 5. Language Understanding, Receptive Language

This Domain addresses the ways in which the participants' understanding of words, sentences, phrases and figures of speech (idioms) influence their relationships and quality of daily activities,

Level 1.0 Typical Development

Participant: Marcus. The participant's language development is "on track". Marcus understands as many words and word combinations as most people in his age group.

The participant reacts or replies when spoken to, and indicates that he has heard the message. When they do not understand a statement they reply with some form of "I don't know".

Marcus and his same-Level peers rarely or hardly ever completely ignore the speaker.

Level 2.0 Minimum/Trace

Participant: Carmen. This participant understands the meaning of fewer words and word-combinations than their peers do. Her overall understanding of language is slightly below that of others in her peer group.

In order to understand the meaning of idioms or figures of speech like "A penny saved is a penny earned" or "Don't cry over spilled milk" the participant may require some supplementary explanation which involve more literal examples of the idiom.

Participants at this Level may not always communicate an "I don't know" statement because they incorrectly assume knowledge of the word or word-combinations.

Participants like Carmen typically do not ignore the speaker, except in instances where that would be appropriate.

Level 3.0 Borderline

Participant: Juan. This participant's understanding of common words, unusual words and word-combinations cover a wide range, varying from slightly below average too much above average.

Juan's main difficulties have to do with idioms and figures of speech. These phrases are incorrectly comprehended as literal statements. Statements such as "All is lost", "That's water under the bridge", or "That dog won't hunt" are often taken literally, and thus misinterpreted. They may not be understood at all.

Juan has difficulty understanding language-based jokes or humor that contains fine points of language. The participants at this Level are more likely than typical persons to not comprehend or to misinterpret the mood or the tone of a conversation.

Level 4.0 Mild

Participant: Raven. Raven's understanding of language varies from slightly below average to considerably below average. It is sometimes difficult to know if she understands the meaning of specific words because she often does not react to the speaker's statement.

When Raven and her same-Level peers were younger than three years old they appeared to not hear sounds. A hearing loss was suspected, and in most cases that problem was put aside after an examination.

Raven remains selective about the words and sounds to which she will react. It is not unusual for the participant to look away when her name is spoken to her, or she simply does not respond.

Level 5.0 Moderate

Participant: Dustin. The participant's understanding of language and receptiveness to spoken language is very limited. He is sometimes able to cooperate when a trusted person makes a simple, direct request for a specific action.

As with Level 4.0 a hearing loss was suspected and in most cases that problem was put aside after an examination.

The participants have little or no understanding of idioms or figures of speech such as "Hop to it", "Break the bank", or "Step up to the plate", and do not achieve long-lasting comprehension even after an explanation.

Dustin reacts to the speaker's statements or questions very hesitantly, and may need several repetitions of the statement in order to reply.

Level 6.0 Severe

Participant: Susana. The participant is severely limited in both the understanding of words, and in making meaningful reactions to other people's spoken language. She offers very little attention to other people's statements or questions.

Susana and her same-Level peers show little or no understanding of complicated sentences. They also show essentially no understanding of figures of speech or idioms such as "Keep your eye on the ball" or "The early bird gets the worm".

The participant's reactions or replies to people's statements are so limited that it is very difficult to identify the difference between what she doesn't know versus what she is simply ignoring. When Susana was younger than three years old she appeared to not hear sounds. A hearing loss was suspected, and in most cases that issue was put aside after an examination.

Susana and other participants at this Level do not always act in response to spoken words and requests alone. The speaker may need to use hands-on guidance and prompts (such as demonstrations and modeling) in order to successfully complete the actions.

Susana only cooperates with or appropriately reacts to a very small number of very familiar trusted people, usually no more than three or four.

Level 7.0 Very Severe

Participant: Scott. For this participant there is almost no observable development of word-understanding or of meaningful reactions to other people's spoken language. Scott offers almost no attention to other people's statements or questions.

Scott and the same-Level participants show no understanding of complicated sentences and no understanding of figures speech or idioms.

The participant offers no reactions or replies to statements made to him by unfamiliar people. In such circumstances there are no practical differences between what is not known versus what is totally ignored.

Scott also does not reply or appropriately react to newly-introduced or spontaneous speech. The statements or phrases to which he might respond are those which have been previously well practiced and rehearsed.

As with participants at the previous Levels, a hearing loss was suspected before the age of three. In most cases that question was put aside after an examination.

Because the participant often does not act in response to spoken words and short-sentence requests alone, the speaker may need to use hands-on guidance and prompts, such as demonstrations and modeling, in order to have the action successfully completed. The speaker may also use American Sign Language and picture boards.

Scott and other participants as his Level offer only a very limited range of cooperation or appropriate reactions to a very small number of very familiar, trusted people, usually no more than two or three.

Domain 6. Social Use of Language, Pragmatic Language

Pragmatic Language describes the <u>style</u> of language and is related to the participant's ability and interest in engaging in a balanced back-and-forth conversation. This Domain covers the ways in which the participants use speech and language in conversations and in social interactions. It also includes the ways in which they change their tone, rate of speech and voice emphasis in their spoken language.

Level 1.0 Typical Development

Participant: Marcus. This participant uses a suitable tone of voice and he accepts guidance and suggestions about his speech from his parents and teachers.

Marcus uses rate of speech, tone and volume (loudness) to appropriately express emotion, such as happiness, excitement, or annoyance.

Statements such as "Please use your inside voice" make sense to Marcus and he can adjust his speaking volume effectively with these types of simple reminders.

Marcus and other participants at this Level have learned the rules of conversation, such as taking turns, being polite, adjusting their conversational style and vocabulary to match the listener, and staying with the topic. They have also learned about waiting while others speak, and about taking turns around one topic in a conversation.

The participant usually speaks politely, and can adjust his speech in order to match the age, ability, and interests of the audience. He is able to engage in a wide variety of conversational topics that is appropriate for his age.

Level 2.0 Minimum/Trace

Participant: Carmen. This participant has some difficulty with adjusting the volume of her voice. In conversation she may be too loud or too soft.

Carmen may have a somewhat flat voice that doesn't express much change in tone or in rate of speaking. It is not always clear whether she is enthusiastic about a topic or not.

The participant may unintentionally interrupt another speaker, or alternately may pause politely while the other person speaks, and then continue with her own sentence as though there were no other conversational partners.

The participant may appear awkward about starting conversations, especially around topics that are mostly social or personal.

Level 3.0 Borderline

Participant: Juan. This participant has some difficulty with using his word knowledge as a resource for relating to people. Teachers and

 Section 4 : On the Level

caregivers may refer to him as "The Young Encyclopedia" because of his expertise in one or more subject areas. Supported by an active curiosity and a great memory, participants at this Level collect great stores of facts on their favorite topics, but are also relatively indifferent to areas in which they have less personal involvement.

When the participant speaks about a preferred topic his tone of voice and rate of speech may appear excited or rushed, as though he is trying to present a large amount of knowledge into one conversational turn. On the other hand, when he joins in a discussion whose topic was chosen by someone else, he might seem hesitant, shy, or speak in a monotone.

The participant is not a very good listener. When he is involved in a conversation he usually talks at the person, rather than with them. He is capable of recognizing and understanding the meaning of what the other people have to say, but he is not very interested in encouraging them to fully express their point of view or knowledge.

Juan and his same-Level participants may very well be kind-hearted and caring people, but they are poor judges of how their statements are being received. They can – and do – say things too people that seem annoying, upsetting, insensitive, or inappropriate. When this happens the participants are often surprised or puzzled by the reaction of the conversational partner. It was not their intention too upset anyone.

Level 4.0 Mild

Participant: Raven. The participant is not interested in conversing about topics other than those of her own choosing. She may ignore attempts to engage her in these conversations, or she may wait for an opening and then abruptly switch to the topic she prefers.

The participant's ability and interest in engaging in a balanced back-and-forth conversation is very limited. When given a choice about speaking she usually prefers to say as little as will allow her to "get by". At other times she might remain silent or simply walk away without giving any explanation for behavior.

These behaviors become especially relevant and influential during adolescence, a time when young people are increasing their social contacts among their peers.

With a great deal of effort, the participant may learn "scripts" which provide the basis or framework for participating in a conversation. This approach is useful for brief conversations, but is rarely able to support conversations that are extensive or detailed.

Raven may not understand nor remember the basic rules of conversation. She may interrupt others, speak over them, or raise her volume above the other speaker's voice. If she pauses when another person speaks, an observer may get the idea that she is not listening with interest, but rather is planning what she will say while she is waiting for her turn to talk.

Level 5.0 Moderate

Participant: Dustin. This participant may speak in a monotone and thus sound "flat", or he may be inappropriately loud or excited. When Dustin speaks it appears to take a lot of effort, and his speech patterns are very different from those of the age-peers whose development is typical.

Dustin does not like too wait his turn, preferring instead to make his statements without regard to the readiness of the listener or the audience. This participant can be blunt and thus appear rude.

Dustin may answer direct questions, but have great difficulty with including another person's statement into his own conversational turn. He is not interested in what other people have to say. The speech of these participants may be sprinkled with sudden changes in the topic, unrelated to the stream of conversation (known as *non sequiturs*).

Other people in their age group do not enjoy speaking with them.

Level 6.0 Severe

Participant: Susana. This participant may avoid using speech to communicate her intentions and ideas, instead relying on physical prompts and cues, such as leading someone by the hand or guiding the person's hand toward the desired object.

Susana and her equal-ability peers may very briefly answer direct questions, but in a manner quite different from other people their age. The reply may vary from a short one-word answer (the bare facts), too an emphatic rejection of the other person's attempts to hold a conversation with them.

Susana is unlikely to engage in conversations with other people.

Level 7.0 Very Severe

Participant: Scott. The communications produced by this participant are very limited, and may seem more like a pre-language style than one of standard language.

Scott is unaware of the subtle nuances of language use - neither his own nor those of others.

He does not want to interact with others, and has considerable difficulty communicating with spoken language about his basic needs or wants.

It is very difficult for other people too know, at a given moment, what this participant needs. The parents, caregivers, or teachers understand that they need to rely on "reading" Scott's spontaneous body language, expressions, and vocalizations.

Domain 7. Body Language, Nonverbal Communication

This Domain covers how well the participant uses and understands non-verbal communication, which is communication based on body language, gestures, facial expressions and eye contact.

Please Note: If the participant's difficulties with body language, gestures, and facial expressions are the result of cerebral palsy or other neurological injury, the understanding of this Domain needs to be modified, and interpreted with considerable caution.

Level 1.0 Typical Development

Participant: Marcus. The participant is able to understand or read body language, gestures, and facial expressions as effectively as his typical peers.

Marcus is able to communicate ideas and feelings as effectively as his peers, using facial expressions, hand movements, body language and gestures.

The participant's hand gestures and facial expressions are coordinated with the spoken statements he is making. The gestures and the words match each other.

Marcus is able too comfortably maintain eye contact with his speaking partners.

He maintains the culturally appropriate physical space during conversation standing neither too close nor too far away.

Level 2.0 Minimum/Trace

Participant: Carmen. She is not quite so skilled as her age- peers at understanding or reading facial expressions, body language, or gestures.

The participant might be somewhat uncertain in using her own facial expressions, body language or gestures to communicate her ideas, emotions, and intentions.

Carmen may prefer a reduced amount of eye contact during a conversation, often looking away from her conversational partner.

She is somewhat less skilled than her peers with easily adjusting the physical space between her and her conversation partner, occasionally under-or-over estimating that space.

Level 3.0 Borderline

Participant: Juan. The consumer often misinterprets body language and gestures, or seem not to notice them at all. For example, he might not distinguish between an expression of concern, versus an expression of fear. Likewise, he might miss the difference between a brief grin and a broad smile.

The participant's own use of facial expressions, body language and gestures are considerably less skilled than others in his age groups.

Juan's natural tendency is to produce fleeting eye contact, rather than the more relaxed, ongoing gaze that takes place in ordinary conversation. When he is reminded about this feature he can usually improve his eye-contact, at least temporarily.

The participant is not very good at judging the proper distance between himself and his conversation partners. He may stand too close, or he may select an awkwardly wide distance between them. In either instance his personal distance is not culturally appropriate, at least at first, before suggestions for correction are accepted.

Level 4.0 Mild

Participant: Raven. The participant at this Level does not know how to receive messages and information from the body language, facial expressions, and gestures produced by other people.

Raven does not intentionally use her own body language too communicate with others.

She avoided looking directly into someone else's eyes even before she was five years old, and this preference continues to the present day. There is very little eye contact and she rarely holds a typical gaze with another person.

Raven may give some attention to a speaker by turning (orienting) her body in the speaker's direction, but at the same time decline too look directly at the speaker's face.

The participant's reluctance to communicate through body language and gestures is basically another aspect of her consistent orientation too minimize communications and interactions with the people in her living-space.

Level 5.0 Moderate

Participant: Dustin. This participant has extreme difficulty understanding facial expressions, body language or gestures. This difficulty continues even when he is provided with coaching, reminders, and hints. He is unable to produce a relevant integrated reaction when he is given the combination of spoken statements and gestured communication. He may even ignore a body language message as straightforward as someone pointing toward a specific object while saying "Look over there".

Dustin does not seem able too intentionally pretend, act, or model an emotion by using body language, facial expressions, or gestures. As a result of these limitations a participant who is nine years old or older does not use or understand the style of sarcasm because facial expressions and gestures play a part in the combination of criticism and humor that convey sarcasm.

Although the participant does not intentionally communicate non-verbally, he may produce a range of body movements, gestures, and facial expressions that express this emotional state. The responsibility for "reading" these patterns rest with the participant's caregiver and other observers.

Dustin prefers a personal space that is much wider than is typical, and the dimensions of this personal space remain fairly constant.

Level 6.0 Severe

Participant: Susana. The participant is unaware of or ignores most of the body language, facial expression, and gestures produced by others. To the extent that spoken language is understood, Susana is more likely to respond too brief, clear, straightforward spoken statements. She can also respond positively too nonverbal communications that involve direct, physical, hands-on guidance, demonstrations, and instructions.

The participant does not use nonverbal communication too express intentions, ideas, or needs, beyond what is seen in basically automatic reactions such as discomfort, anger, fright, laughter, fascination, or rejection of something.

Susana and her equally-capable peers prefer to have a lot of space between themselves and another person, and they consistently avoid eye contact, turning away when another person looks directly at them.

Level 7.0 Very Severe

Participant: Scott. He does not notice body language, facial expressions and gestures of other people. He does not intentionally use body language, facial expressions, and gestures to communicate his own ideas, intentions and needs.

Scott does not engage in conversation and does not attend to the speaker. He works energetically too avoid personal interactions and eye contact.

Scott avoids interaction or withdraws when other people get close to entering his personal space. If withdrawing from interaction is inconvenient, he might aggressively push away other people.

Domain 8. Flexibility & Transitions

This Domain covers the participants' interest in new experiences - whether they prefer a wide range of activities or a constant routine. This Domain also covers how comfortably the participants can transition from one activity too another.

Level 1.0 Typical Development

Participant: Marcus. The participant learns new ideas, activities, and games easily and naturally.

He plays a variety of games with others, including rule-based and make-believe games. He can adapt to changes in rules or play as they happen, and rarely engages in arguments over the rules of play.

Marcus learns the rules for all aspects of daily life (crossing the street, playing games, engaging in conversation) while maintaining an awareness about when the situation requires modifying those rules. This flexibility becomes the basis for effectively adjusting too new and changing circumstances.

He is able to fit into the life around him and "go with the flow".

Marcus understands that objects can have several uses, such as using a shoe as a makeshift hammer, or a chair as a temporary ladder.

When Marcus is engaged in an activity, even a favorite one, and is asked too transition too something else, he can do it easily and pleasantly - most of the time.

When his surroundings change slightly (such as a new picture in the hallway or the rearrangement of furniture), these changes may not be noticed. If they are noticed Marcus regards them as unimportant.

Level 2.0 Minimum/Trace

Participant: Carmen. The participant may prefer routines throughout the day. Established routines are the structure upon which she relies for getting through the day. Routines are the pathways for daily activities such as getting ready for school, preparing the table for dinner, getting ready for bed, etc.

She may need to be coached about what to expect before beginning a new experience such as getting on an airplane, going to the beach, or changing to a different school.

Carmen feels comfortable when games have clearly-defined rules, and may seem a little lost with free-form play or activities that rely on imagination and fantasy.

This participant is more likely than the typical person too has difficulty changing her mind once she has decided on an opinion. Some people might describe her as "rigid" in her thinking.

The participant can seem bothered or upset when asked to change activities. She may take extra time to finish with one activity before being willing to move on to the next one.

These preferences for routine and constancy sometimes present inconveniences and challenges to the participant, her caregivers and her teachers. However, on the whole these preferences do not seriously disrupt the events of daily life.

Level 3.0 Borderline

Participant: Juan. He expresses a preference for games that have clearly-defined rules. He usually does not ask to be included in creative, free-form play with other people, and other people usually do not invite him too join them.

The participant may show a lack of flexibility in his thinking or problem-solving skills. He is reluctant to change an idea or concept that he has accepted as correct, even when new information is introduced. For this reason, misunderstandings are hard to change, and often seem "set in stone".

Juan is bothered or upset when suddenly asked to change activities, and may even have tantrums. He often appreciates a five-minute warning before being asked to transition from one activity to the next.

The participant's lack of flexibility and difficulty with transitions sometimes presents challenges too family members and friends, who are asked to be especially patient, considerate, and creative in dealing with these characteristics.

Level 4.0 Mild

Participant: Raven. This participant places a definite emphasis on a known routine and a predictable schedule. Her ability to transition between activities benefits greatly from consistent practice and rehearsal of that transition schedule.

Raven's constructive cooperative behavior is shaped by rules that were learned with considerable effort by her, and taught with considerable effort by her caregivers, teachers, and other family members. It is very difficult for Raven too understand that these rules can be modified, and indeed that it may sometimes be necessary to make those changes. The participant may be bothered by what would ordinarily be small changes in her home environment, such as a new picture on the wall or the rearrangement of furniture.

Raven directs her attention to a specific, sharply-focused activity, and is very reluctant to leave that activity and move on to another.

Parents and caregivers have learned too adapt their schedules and daily activities to meet the participant's need for constancy and routine. Her need for constancy may be evident in the way she resists changes in the day's schedule. She may react poorly too changes in the time at which dinner is eaten, or the time set aside for TV viewing.

The participant has noticeable difficulty making transitions from one situation or event too another. She requires more than a five-minute advance notice in order to cooperate with a previously unplanned transition. She may require more advance notice, some additional reminders, or the offer of a reward.

Level 5.0 Moderate

Participant: Dustin. He is deeply attached to his daily routines, behavior rituals and repetitions. He does not cope well when his routine is changed. When things do not happen in the expected order he is likely to become angry or agitated. He may temporarily refuse to cooperate or he may engage in self-hurting behaviors.

The participant shows great inflexibility in thinking and problem-solving. He depends on sameness in most aspects of his life - the same foods, the same desk, the same schedule, the same activities.

Major changes in the participant's life, such as changes in his classroom, school, neighborhood, doctor, or family vacation plans often result in major "meltdowns". Parents, caregivers and teachers need to do considerable pre-teaching in order to reduce such incidents.

Level 6.0 Severe

Participant: Susana. She has developed a complex and extensive set of personal routines and rules. These rules are used to organize and govern most, if not all aspects of her daily life. Susana insists on doing the same thing in the same way each time.

She requires of her day that each activity and each transition be identified so that she can anticipate and plan for the change. This schedule may be in writing or represented by pictures.

Susana may refuse too transition from a familiar activity too an unexpected "off-schedule" one. Her distress may result in a tantrum.

Changes in the way things are done, alterations in the order of daily events, or even changes in the arrangement of the furniture can - and do - cause emotional outbursts or other intense negative reactions.

Level 7.0 Very Severe

Participant: Scott. The participant is extremely immersed and focused on his routines, procedures, behavior rituals and personal interests. These routines and personal interests are the ruling realities of his life. They push aside just about every other activity or possible experience. He has no interests in exploring other activities, places, events, or skills. A very narrow range of repeated activity occupies his waking hours.

Scott firmly and energetically resists changes too his self-selected routines. His resistance can be silently unmoving or actively angry and protesting, even to the point of becoming aggressive.

Any attempt to introduce slight changes in activities, new people, or small changes in his routine must be done very thoughtfully, slowly, and with great skill over an extended span of time.

Domain 9. Repeating Body Movements, Movement Stereotypes

This Domain covers how often the participant engages in unusual, repeating body movements

If the participant's difficulties with body movements and gestures are the result of cerebral palsy or neurological injury, the understanding of this section should be modified and interpreted with considerable caution.

Level 1.0 Typical Development

Participant: Marcus. His body movements, gestures, and facial expressions are similar to those of other people in his age group.

When Marcus is very excited or tense he may show some movement spill-over. This _temporarily_ agitated state can include movements such as jumping up and down, bouncing in a chair, brief flapping of the hands, or pumping the arms in a victory gesture. These behaviors usually fade away when the participant calms down.

The participant transitions his body movements smoothly from one activity too another. His body movements are right and effective for the activity in progress, such as walking, running, bicycle riding, dancing, gymnastics, or moving back and forth on a playground swing.

Marcus does not engage in self-hurting acts such as head-banging, punching or slapping of himself, or hand-biting. There may be a small amount of fingernail biting.

Level 2.0 Minimum/Trace

Participant: Carmen. This participant is not quite so skillful with fine and large muscle activities as most people of her age.

Carmen is more likely than most of her age-peers too do some small repeating behaviors such as tapping her fingers or feet, pacing back and forth, or brushing her hair.

She developed a preference for either the right or left hand somewhat later than most children. Her handwriting, especially cursive, is less clear than the writing of other people in her age-group.

The participant usually has some favorite object she likes to hold and manipulate, such as a wristwatch, pencil, decorative pin, necklace, or jacket button.

Carmen does not intentionally strike her head against hard objects, nor does she hit or bite herself. She does not produce other self-hurting behaviors (normal accidents are excluded).

Level 3.0 Borderline

Participant: Juan. He had, and may still have some difficulty with large-muscle coordination and balance. Juan had challenges with learning to do things like ride a bicycle, skate, catch a ball, or walk a balance beam.

He also had difficulty with fine-muscle coordination and was less skillful than others in his age group with actions like fastening buttons, working zippers, picking up small marbles, or handing a deck of playing cards.

When this participant is excited or stressed he may flap or wring his hands, rock back and forth, or pinch his clothing. These repeating body movements usually do <u>not</u> happen every day. He may also produce unusual facial grimaces or tics, but these also do not happen every day.

The participant does not intentionally strike his head against hard objects, nor does he hit or bite himself. He does not produce other self-hurting behaviors (normal accidents not included).

Level 4.0 Mild

Participant; Raven. At this Level the participant produces one or more of the unusual repeating movements listed below, which typically happen every day. Some of the behaviors may happen several times each day. The behaviors are:

1. Walking on tip-toes
2. Whirling or turning in a circle
3. Flapping of the hands
4. Rocking back-and-forth, either while sitting or standing
5. Wiggling or flicking the fingers
6. Slapping the side of the body.

These repetitive movements may briefly interrupt Raven's activities, and distract others who are around her. However, these unusual behaviors are <u>not</u> so frequent or so severe that they seriously disrupt the continuity of her activities or schedule.

Raven does not intentionally strike her head against hard objects, nor does she hit or bite herself. She does not produce other self-hurting behaviors (normal accidents are excluded).

Level 5.0 Moderate

Participant: Dustin He produces two or more kinds of the unusual repeating movements listed below. He may engage in these movements 6 too 9 times each day. As listed above, the behaviors are:

1. Walking on tip-toes
2. Whirling or turning in a circle
3. Flapping of the hands
4. Rocking back-and-forth, either while sitting or standing
5. Wiggling or flicking the fingers
6. Slapping the side of the body

These repetitive movements are frequent and severe enough too significantly interrupt the continuity of his activities and schedule.

While these movements may convey tension, discomfort, anxiety, annoyance or anger, they are not

the usual kinds of gestures and facial expressions
with which most people communicate.

The participant might engage in serious self-hurting
behaviors such as hitting himself or intentionally
striking his head. These behaviors might happen 1 or
2 times per week, and can result in serious bodily
injury.

Level 6.0 Severe

Participant: Susana. She produces three or more
types of the unusual, repeating movements listed
below, as often as 10 too 15 times per day. These
incidents are wide-spread and ongoing. As previously
stated, the behaviors are:

1. Walking on tip-toes
2. Whirling or turning in a circle
3. Flapping of the hands
4. Rocking back-and-forth, either while sitting or
    standing
5. Wiggling or flicking the fingers
6. Slapping the side of the body

These repetitive movements are intense and severe
enough too seriously disrupt and interfere with
Susana's activities and schedule.

In some cases, the frequency and intensity of the
participant's self-hurting behaviors can make it
necessary to use protective clothing and accessories,
such as gloves and protective headgear.

Level 7.0 Very Severe

Participant: Scott This participant produces 3 or more types of the unusual, repeating movements listed below, as often as 16 too 30 times per day. On some days they may be even more frequent. These incidents are wide-spread and ongoing.

1. Walking on tip-toes
2. Whirling or turning in a circle
3. Flapping of the hands
4. Rocking back-and-forth, either while sitting or standing
5. Wiggling or flicking the fingers
6. Slapping the side of the body

Scott's repeating movements and self-hurting behaviors are nearly constant, and tend to dominate his activities and schedule.

The frequency and intensity of these behaviors make it very difficult to engage him in useful or productive activities. The conditions for achieving school-based learning are very challenging.

The nature of Scott's self-hurting behaviors can make it necessary to use protective clothing and accessories, such as gloves and protective headgear.

Domain 10. Creative Imagination

This Domain covers the participants' use of imagination in their daily activities. It also covers the extent to which the participant interacts with the tangible physical properties of objects, rather than making use of the functionality and concepts represented by the object.

(Time-frame note: Most of the following descriptions address the behaviors as though they are happening in present time. Please assume that the descriptions also apply too behaviors that happened in the past.)

Level 1.0 Typical Development

Participant: Marcus. By the time Marcus was three years old he recognized that small toys, such as action figures, dolls, dollhouses, animals, cars and trucks all represented something larger in the world.

The participant did not treat the toys and figures simply as objects without meaning, but correctly viewed them as models that had been scaled down for children's use and imaginative play.

Marcus could use the toys and action figures to construct an imaginary story. He could also be a player in little imaginative dramas and games with other children.

By the age of four, Marcus was participating in and enjoying make-believe games and role playing.

The participant has no difficulty with imagining events or possibilities that are not immediately in front of him. He also uses imagination as a resource for creativity, constructive planning, social interaction, and entertainment.

Level 2.0 Minimum/Trace

Participant: Carmen. The participant may use small toys such as action figures, dolls, animals, or cars too tell a story. However, the story is likely to be a re-telling of one already known to the participant, rather than an example of a mostly original idea or script.

The participant is not drawn too activities that emphasize fantasy, vivid imagination, or speculation, especially if they appear too have no useful purpose. She is unlikely to seek out make-believe games or role-playing dramas.

Carmen applies her creativity and imagination towards activities and projects that are practical, reasonable, and possibly useful. She is not a dreamer, but rather a very down-to-earth and realistic person.

She prefers to do things whose outcomes can be anticipated and which are achievable, such as working on math problems, learning the lines of an already-written play, or drawing pictures that are clear and realistic.

Level 3.0 Borderline

Participant: Juan. He is more likely than his peers too prefer independent or solo imaginative play. He is able to use action figures, dolls, and toys for his own make-believe play in much the same way as the typical child. However, he encounters difficulty with <u>shared</u> imaginative play.

On those occasions in which cooperative or shared imaginative play is attempted with other children, the story line does not fit well. His playmates are often puzzled or confused by the way in which his story-line doesn't build on or connect to the story-line produced by the other children.

The participant limits his make-believe games and creativity too one or two preferred subjects, and has difficulty creating other story lines.

He is usually more interested in the practical ways in which an object works than he is in the appearance of the object, or the way this object fits into its surroundings.

Juan has some difficulty imagining what another person's point of view might be.

Level 4.0 Mild

Participant: Raven. She can name or identify her various toys or action figures (cowboy, police officer, fire-fighter, dancer, magician, dollhouse, etc.) but she does not create any stories or make-believe dramas with them.

Raven is interested in the physical appearance of her toys, such as their shape, color, size, or texture. The toys are arranged, lined up, or stacked in a specific way, often on the basis of those physical features.

This participant either did not develop imaginative play and make-believe stories, or these were expressed in a very limited way. The use of imagination plays only a very small part in her daily life. She goes through her day based mostly on what has been well learned, and on what can be clearly seen, heard, touched or tasted.

She has little or no interest in speculation, conjecture, or in trying to imagine possibilities that she has not already experienced. Visual aids are useful when discussing abstract concepts. For example, a discussion of "next week" or "next month" would benefit from a calendar so that these participants can see the number of days that are involved.

Level 5.0 Moderate

Participant: Dustin. He has some difficulty with naming or identifying his various toys or action figures. He does not use these playthings too express a story line or an imaginative drama. He is interested in the physical appearance of his toys and possessions, such as their shape, color, size, or texture. He arranges, lines up, or stacks these possessions on the basis of their physical features.

This participant did not develop imaginative play or make-believe stories. He does not participate in imaginative games or make-believe dramas with other children, and has no interest in doing so. His thinking and behavior are directed towards the physical objects that are immediately in front of him.

Dustin is not able to use imagination as a resource for creativity, constructive planning or relaxation. He has very strong preferences for a known and predictable routine.

He needs and develops behavioral rituals that go far beyond the kinds of routine activities that are valued by most people.

Level 6.0 Severe

Participant: Susana. She may arrange, collect, or stack objects based on physical features such as size, color, shape or texture.

Susana did not develop any solo imaginative play, does not engage in any cooperative imaginative play, and shows no interest in doing so. The development and expression of imaginative ideas or creative thinking are not part of her daily activities.

She is deeply committed to her daily routines and behavior rituals, and can become very upset and agitated if these routines are changed in any way.

The participant's highly ritualized behaviors are minimally connected too, or influenced by other people. The rituals are not intended to be useful too her family, school, or community.
For this participant and others at the same Level, the absence of imagination and the creative problem-solving abilities which imagination promotes make it

extremely difficult - if not impossible - for them to deal effectively with new and possibly unsafe situations.

Level 7.0 Very Severe

Participant: Scott. He shows many of the same behaviors as someone who is at Level 6.0, but his overall range of functioning is even more limited. Rather than playing with objects as symbols, models or imaginative characters he uses them in a highly ritualized and unusual way. For instance, he may rub the soft covering of a teddy bear against his cheek, over and over, but not imaginatively pretend that the teddy bear can role play.

Scott never developed imaginative play nor did he produce make-believe stories, either independently or in cooperation with someone else. His daily activities are mostly determined by what is immediately in front of him.

Scott does not use imagination as a resource and does not engage in creative thinking or constructive problem-solving. He does not engage in shared fantasies or imaginative stories with anyone.

He might be able to understand the concept of "tomorrow". However, he is likely to need additional explanation in order to understand time concepts that go much beyond "tomorrow".

Domain 11. Imitation & Empathy

This Domain covers the participants' ability to understand someone else's feelings, intentions, and experiences, and also covers their ability to imitate the behavior of others.

Level 1.0 Typical Development

Participant: Marcus. When he observes an action or a series of actions he is able to attempt an imitation or repetition of those actions. Becoming successful with the repetition usually requires practice.

The knowledge and skills acquired by the participant make up an important part of his language, social, mental and school-based effectiveness.

The capacity for empathy displayed by Marcus is seen when he is able to "put himself in someone else's shoes".

Marcus is able to understand some of the ways in which another person might think about and react too some events, as long as those events are within the range of his own personal experiences.

Level 2.0 Minimum/Trace

Participant: Carmen. She can observe an action or a series of actions and is then able to attempt an imitation or repetition of those actions. However, she might require more time and practice than the typical participant in order to be successful.

She is able to "put herself in someone else's shoes", but not so easily or as fully as the typical participant of her age.

Carmen can understand how another person might think about or experience some event, but requires additional explanation and discussion in order to reach that understanding.

Level 3.0 Borderline

Participant: Juan He can imitate or copy most of the straightforward, uncomplicated actions and language that he observes.

However, he is less skillful in using imitation too learn the fine points and subtle variations of social interaction, styles of speaking, and polite behavior. He may not recognize that a situation requires a different approach, a new alternative, or an exception to the usual rule.

Juan has some difficulty with "putting himself into someone else's shoes". For example, when he is talking with someone he may be unaware that the other person wishes to speak, or that a listener might be bored or annoyed with him.

Level 4.0 Mild

Participant: Raven. Her ability to imitate and copy behavior is significantly under-developed. She learns basic social conduct and conventions more slowly and with more effort than her typical peers.

The ability to imitate spoken sounds and words is significantly decreased, resulting in large delays in the development of speech and language.

Raven has only a very basic ability to intuitively recognize and understand someone else's intentions or feelings.

Given very purposeful, concentrated instruction Raven can identify major conditions that produce happiness or sadness, satisfaction or disappointment, safety or danger. However, she is usually not interested in recognizing the subtler or shaded emotional states in other people. She usually does not understand that another person feels embarrassed, annoyed, disappointed or anxious.

Level 5.0 Moderate

Participant: Dustin. This participant's ability to imitate and copy behavior is under-developed in major ways. He learns basic social conduct and conventions much more slowly and considerably less completely than typical participants.

Dustin's ability to imitate spoken sounds and the words that are built from these sounds is dramatically lessened, resulting in widespread impairment in his ability to acquire speech and language.

The participant's capacity to intuitively recognize and understand someone else's intentions and feelings is present in only a very fragmentary form.

Dustin is mostly focused on his own thoughts, emotions, sensations, movements and personal involvements. He has little-to-no interest in another person's emotional condition or thoughts.

Level 6.0 Severe

Participant: Susana. The participant's ability to imitate and copy behavior is drastically under-developed to the point of being almost entirely absent. She learns basic social conduct and conventions very slowly and very incompletely. Her ability to imitate spoken sounds and the words that are built from those sounds is severely under-developed to the point where there is little or no clearly spoken language.

Susana requires ongoing, steady guidance, support, and instruction in order to progress through a daily schedule. Her capacity to intuitively recognize and understand someone else's intentions, feelings, or desires is either completely absent or present in only a minimal way. She concentrates her attention on her own thoughts, feelings, sensations and movements.

She has essentially no interest in another person's experiences or wishes.

Level 7.0 Very Severe

Participant: Scott. His ability to imitate and copy behavior is present to only the smallest extent. He is able to move through his daily schedule only with the application of ongoing, steady guidance, support and coaching.

He learns the general outline of the day's activities and can retain this learning for a brief time, perhaps a few days or weeks. However, unless the guidance, support and coaching are continued regularly, the learning will be lost and he will slide into a completely non-interactive, self-occupied condition.

Scott is unable to imitate spoken sounds and the words that are built from those sounds. As a result, he has no clearly spoken language.

He focuses his attention on his own thoughts, feelings, sensations, movements and needs. It is only with direct, close face-to-face communication and hands-on guidance and directions that he will briefly focus on another person or re-direct his attention.

When left to his own preferences he has no awareness of and no interest in another person's experiences, wishes, moods, or plans.

Domain 12. Unusual Sensory Events

This Domain covers extreme reactions to sensory input. These may include sounds, discomfort with being touched, and fascination with different textures, extreme sensitivity to smell and aromas, unusual reactions to changing patterns of light and flickering light, fascination with the feel of flowing water, unusual reactions to discomfort or pain, and others.

Level 1.0 Typical Development

Participant: Marcus. He is quite open to exploring a wide range of textures, sights, sounds and tastes.

As a young child he learned about his surroundings partly through touch and taste, and is open to trying new activities, touching new materials, and trying new tastes.

While Marcus may have preferences in clothing styles, he is willing to wear a wide variety of materials and usually does not experience seams and tags as uncomfortable or annoying.

He is as comfortable with a light tickle as with a bear hug. He can move easily between a darkened room and bright sunshine, and is not particularly bothered by most sounds. The everyday experience of a wide variety of sights, sounds, textures, tastes and skin pressures blend smoothly into the ongoing activities of the day.

Marcus does not "get lost" in a sensory experience, and he does <u>not</u> use the sensory activity to replace the usual activities, friendships, and social interactions of his community.

He does not show extreme discomfort with the kinds of sensory experiences that are ordinary for most people.

Level 2.0 Minimum/Trace

Participant: Carmen. She is more sensitive than most people to some textures. She may dislike certain materials touching her skin such as velvet, burlap or wool. She may also dislike foods or liquids such as oatmeal, smoothies, carrots or other crunchy foods.

Carmen may have a negative reaction to certain sounds, and they may cause her to pull away. The unwanted sounds may annoy her the same way others might be bothered by fingernails on a chalkboard or a squeaky balloon.

She may be more than usually sensitive to certain smells.

This participant does <u>not</u> replace friendships and social activity with sensory stimulation.

Level 3.0 Borderline

Participant: Juan. He can be very particular and demanding about sensory experiences and materials.

The participant may remove all the tags and labels from his shirts because the slight thickness bothers him. He may insist on wearing socks inside-out, or prefer to wear no socks at all.

He may avoid certain materials such as denim, velvet or wool. He may prefer very loose-fitting clothing.

Juan may also have strong dislikes in food textures as well as some odors.

He may prefer certain types of lighting. He may complain of headaches at school and need to wear a baseball cap or sunglasses in rooms that have fluorescent lighting. He may even dislike the distinctive buzzing sound produced by those fluorescent lights.

This participant does not usually replace friendships and social interactions with simple sensory stimulation. However, he may have a strong interest in filling large portions of his time with complicated sensory stimulation such as video games.

If Juan has an interest in or talent for music, he might practice or play music for long spans of time.

Level 4.0 Mild

Participant: Raven. She shows an attraction to certain kinds of sensory stimulation and an aversion to others.

Raven may be fascinated by patterns of flickering lights and may produce a similar sensation by flicking or flapping her fingers in front of her eyes.

She may appear to not hear some ordinary sounds and later may cover her ears in an attempt to block out a slightly different sound.

She can focus on or become immersed in the experience of simple sensory stimulation. The sensory input can come from a variety of sources, including the sensation of water from a faucet flowing over her hands, the sensation of muscle movements while rocking back and forth, the experience of the textures of various kinds of cloths, and patterns of light or music.

If left to her own preferences the participant will allow sensory stimulation to replace friendships, social interaction, and shared activities.

Level 5.0 Moderate

Participant: Dustin. At this Level the participant's attraction to and rejection of certain forms of sensory stimulation is sharply divided. He seeks out a great deal of sensory stimulation that does not involve relating to people or participating in shared activities. He will also avoid or energetically reject other kinds of sensory experiences.

Dustin and his Same-Level peers seek out a wide variety of sensory stimulation, which may include any of those listed:

1. Carrying a favorite object.
2. Spinning an object and staring at it.
3. Sniffing or smelling objects.
4. Tasting or licking objects that are not food.
5. Flicking or flapping fingers in front of the eyes.
6. Staring at changing patterns of lights.
7. Stimulation by body movements, such as rocking back-and-forth.
8. The stimulation that comes from hitting oneself.
9. Repeating words and phrases over and over.
10. Producing sounds that are not standard words.
11. Rubbing the hands over some kind of texture such as carpets, terrycloth, silk, or smooth hard surfaces.

There can be as many as 12 episodes a day for any of these behaviors.

Dustin also strongly rejects certain stimuli, including physical contact with other people. He does not like to be touched or held by another person. He might cover his ears with his hands in an effort to shut out certain sounds.

The participant rejects a wide range of food choices, settling on a very narrow menu.

He might have no reaction at all to small cuts or bruises.

This pattern of sensory fascination and rejection presents major obstacles to social relationships, participation in ordinary activities and the constructive experience of education.

Level 6.0 Severe

Participant: Susana. Her sensory fascinations and rejections are intense and forceful.

Susana seeks out a wide variety of sensory stimulation, which may include–but are not limited to–the collection of methods that are listed above in Level 5.0.

There can be as many as 16 episodes a day for any of these behaviors.

Susana rejects many forms of sensory stimulation. The rejection is often forceful and sometimes aggressive. She rejects physical contact, eye contact, some food textures, and can also reject some textures in clothing and furnishings.

The participant may refuse to walk barefoot, finger paint or wear clothing of specific materials. She may gag at certain odors and may have extremely sensitive hearing or vision issues, especially about fluorescent lights. She may insist on wearing sunglasses.

The combination of intense fascinations and aggressive avoidance this participant shows for certain sensory stimuli present large obstacles for her. These energetic reactions make it even more difficult for her to form friendly interactive relationships, acquire skills and knowledge through education, and participate meaningfully in her community.

Level 7.0 Very Severe

Participant: Scott. All of the sensory fascinations and rejections that are described in Levels 5.0 and 6.0 are also seen with this participant, at this Level.

There can be 20 or more episodes a day for any of these behaviors.

The intense fascinations and aggressive avoidance Scott shows for certain sensory stimuli pose very large and persistent obstacles for him. These extreme reactions work against the formation of pleasant social relationships, the acquisition of skill and knowledge through education, and meaningful participation in his community.

An Invitation

Dear Reader,

We invite your opinion about any aspect of this
book, including if you found it helpful, accurate, or
informative.

We also invite your participation in a research
study designed to validate a survey form to be used
in the identification and progress monitoring of
children who may be on the autism spectrum.

The survey is called the Continuum of Autism
Spectrum Traits (C.O.A.S.T.) and examines a
child's patterns of abilities in the twelve domains
presented in this book.

To provide feedback or to learn more about
participating in the validation study, please email
Kim Sherman at kim.otbc@gmail.com

Section 5.
The Rotated Matrix Orientation.

In this method of presentation, the seven Levels of Severity are presented, in turn, as the main topic. The characteristics of each of the Twelve Domains that correspond to the selected Level of Severity are displayed in their previously arranged (Section 4) numerical sequence.

This arrangement of the material allows the reader to concurrently examine the influence (or impact) of a given Level of Severity on multiple areas of functioning.

Note: Please recall that we have linked each one of the Levels of Severity to the name of a fictitious participant. These linkages between the fictitious name of the participant and the Level are consistent across all twelve Domains. Marcus is always at Level 1.0, Juan is always at Level 3.0, and so forth. This consistency of presentation is used in order to promote ease of discussion about the Levels among the readers of *On The Level*. A second reason for this arrangement is the assumption that the consistency of linkage helps the reader to learn about the features of the various Levels more efficiently.

With that said we wish to emphasize that in actual practice, in "real life", a participant can behave, function, and think at more than one Level on various domains and can **change over time** as a result of maturity, skill building, and direct instruction. A person's Level of functioning is **not frozen** at a single point. It is also unlikely that a person's skills will be at the same Level over all twelve Domains. Most participants will typically show variability in their profile, with strengths and challenges in particular Domains.

Level 1.0 Typical Development for Age. (Neurotypical).

No significant or distinctive autism traits have been observed. This zone of the autism spectrum does not show any prominent autism-related deficits or excesses. However, Domain functioning at Level 1.0 does not exclude the possibility of the presence of other mental health issues.

Participant: Marcus

Domain 1. Social Relationships.

The participant's social relationships, friendships and interactions are typical for someone of his age. He looks for friendships and is usually successful in finding them. Alternately, if he is not actively seeking relationships then he is open to developing new ones. Marcus places a high value on being understood and accepted by other people.

Marcus joins in and participates in various group activities. When participating in these activities he understands both the obvious spelled-out rules and the unstated background rules. These two areas of rules can be described as the explicit rules for the activity, and the rules for behaving in the context in which the activity takes place.

The participants at this Level are emotionally connected to some or all of the members of their family, and they very much value their place in the family network.

Domain 2. Language Expression.

The participant's language expression abilities are "on track". He is able to speak as many words and word-combinations as most other people in his age group. His use of spoken language is nicely balanced with his ability to understand the statement made by other people. Both of these skills are at an expected level of achievement for Marcus' age-peers.

By the time Marcus was four years old he could say his name and age, develop friendships, sing songs and recite nursery rhymes. Participants who are at least six years old can tell stories, discuss events, and talk about their plans for some future activities such as a birthday party, vacation, camping trip, visit to a theme part, or visit to another family. Marcus is able to speak about plans in ways that are more detailed and elaborate than just a simple statement of one or two facts.

Domain 3. Types of Interests.

The participant developed his skills and learned about his surroundings by sampling a wide variety of activities and experiences. He welcomes the opportunity to explore aspects of his environment. He likes to share his interests and activities with other people. Importantly, other people serve as an audience that offers encouragement, approval, and guidance for improvement. The adults of the community also set boundaries and procedures that promote safety.

Marcus enjoys learning about a wide variety of topics, and experiences satisfaction and pride from increasing his inventory of knowledge and from recognizing the improvements in his range of useful skills.

Domain 4. Personal Management and Self-Direction.

The participant is able to design, arrange and manage his activities and materials as effectively as others in his age group. He is able to show a reasonable amount of emotional self-restraint when facing some challenges.

The participant is an effective self-starter and is not overwhelmed at the prospect of starting a project or engaging a series of responsibilities. He can smoothly transition to another activity when the job is completed or the time is up.

The participant is able to stay focused on the job at hand, and disregards or screens-out irrelevant, potentially distracting events. He has learned how to review, track, and evaluate his work or activities as he goes along. With that awareness in place he is able to effectively self-correct or adjust his efforts in a timely way.

Domain 5. Language Understanding. Receptive Language.

The participant's language development is "on track" Marcus understands as many words and word combinations as most people in his age group. He reacts or replies when spoken to, and indicates that he has heard the message. When he does not understand a statement he replies with some form of "I don't know" communication.

Marcus and his Same-Level peers rarely or hardly ever completely ignore the speaker.

Domain 6. Social Use of Language. Pragmatic Language.

This Domain addresses the ways in which the participants use speech and language in conversations and in social interactions. The participant uses a suitable tone of voice. He accepts guidance and suggestions about his speech from his parents and teachers. Marcus uses rate of speech, tone and volume (loudness) to appropriately express emotion, such as happiness, excitement, or annoyance.

Statements such as "Please use your inside voice" make sense to Marcus and he can adjust his speaking volume effectively when given these types of simple reminders.

Marcus and other participants at this Level have learned the rules of conversation, such as taking turns, being polite, adjusting their conversational style and vocabulary to match the listener, and staying with the topic. They have also learned about waiting while others speak, and about taking turns around one topic in a conversation.

The participant usually speaks politely, and can adjust his speech in order to match the age, ability, and interests of the audience. He is able to engage in a wide variety of conversational topics that are appropriate for his age.

Domain 7. Body Language. Nonverbal Communication.

If the participant's difficulties with body language, gestures, and facial expressions are the result of cerebral palsy or other neurological injury, the understanding of this Domain needs to be modified, and interpreted with considerable caution.

He is able to understand or read body language, gestures, and facial expressions, hand movements, body language and gestures. The participant's hand gestures and facial expressions are coordinated with the spoken statements he is making. The gestures and the words match each other.

Marcus is able to comfortably maintain eye contact with his speaking partners. He maintains the culturally appropriate physical space during conversation, standing neither too close nor too far away.

Domain 8. Flexibility and Transitions.

This Domain addresses the participants' interest in new experiences - whether they prefer a wide range of activities or a narrow constant routine. This Domain also covers how comfortably the participants can transition from one activity to another.

He learns new ideas, activities and games easily and naturally. He plays a variety of games with others, including rule-based and make-believe games. He can adapt to changes in rules or play as they happen, and rarely engages in arguments over the rules of play.

Marcus learns the rules for all aspects of daily life (crossing the street, playing games, engaging in conversation) while maintaining an awareness about when the situation requires modifying those rules. This flexibility becomes the basis for effectively adjusting to new and changing circumstances.

He is able to fit into the life around him and "go with the flow". Marcus understands that objects can have several uses, such as using a shoe as a makeshift hammer, or a chair as a temporary ladder. When Marcus is engaged in an activity, even a favorite one, and is asked to transition to something else, he can do it easily and pleasantly - most of the time.

When his surroundings change slightly (such as a new picture in the hallway or the rearrangement of furniture) these changes may not be noticed. If they are noticed Marcus regards them as unimportant.

Domain 9. Repeating Body Movements. Movement Stereotypes.

This Domain discusses how often the participant engages in unusual repeating body movements.

If the participant's difficulties with body language, gestures, and facial expressions are the result of cerebral palsy or other neurological injury, the understanding of this Domain needs to be modified, and interpreted with considerable caution.

The participant's body movements, gestures, and facial expressions are similar to those of other people in his age group. When Marcus is very excited or tense he may show some movement spill-over. This temporary agitated state can include movements such as jumping up and down, bouncing in a chair, brief flapping of the hands, or pumping the arms in a victory gesture. These behaviors usually fade away when the participant calms down.

The participant transitions his body movements smoothly from one activity to another. His body movements are right and effective for the activity in progress, such as walking, running, bicycle riding, dancing, gymnastics, or moving back and forth on a playground swing.

He does not engage in self-hurting acts such as head-banging, punching or slapping of himself, or hand-biting. There may be a small amount of fingernail biting.

Domain 10. Creative Imagination.

This Domain covers the participants' use of imagination in their daily activities, as well as the extent to which the participant interacts with the tangible physical properties of objects, rather than making use of the functionality and concepts presented by the object. *(Time-frame note. Most of the following descriptions address the behaviors as though they are happening in present time. Please assume that the descriptions also apply to behaviors that happened in the past.)*

By the time Marcus was three years old he recognized that small toys, such as action figures, dolls, dollhouses, animals, cars and trucks all represented something larger in the world. The participant did not treat the toys and figures simply as objects without meaning, but correctly viewed them as models that had been scaled down for children's use and imaginative play.

Marcus could use the toys and action to construct an imaginary story. He could also be a player in little imaginative dramas and games with other children. By the age of four, Marcus was participating in and enjoying make-believe games and role-playing.

The participant has no difficulty with imagining events or possibilities that are no immediately in front of him. He also uses imagination as a resource for creativity, constructive planning, social interaction and entertainment.

Domain 11. Imitation and Empathy.

When Marcus observes an action or a series of actions he is able to attempt an imitation or repetition of those actions. Becoming successful with the repetition usually requires practice. The knowledge and skills acquired by the participant make up an important part of his language, social, mental and school-based effectiveness.

The capacity for empathy displayed by Marcus is seen when he is able to "put himself in someone else's shoes". He is able to understand some of the ways in which another person might think about and react to some events, as long as those events are within the range of his own personal experiences.

Domain 12. Unusual Sensory Events.

The participant is quite open to exploring a wide range of textures, sights, sounds and tastes. As a young child Marcus learned about his surroundings partly through touch and taste, and is open to trying new activities, touching new materials and trying new tastes. While he may have preferences in clothing styles he is willing to wear a wide variety of materials and usually does not experience seams and tags as uncomfortable or annoying.

He is as comfortable with a light tickle as with a bear hug. He can move easily between a darkened room and bright sunshine, and is not particularly bothered by most sounds. The everyday experience of a wide variety of sights, sounds, textures, tastes and skin pressures all blend smoothly into the ongoing activities of the day.

Marcus does not "get lost" in a sensory experience, and he does <u>not</u> use the sensory activity to replace the usual activities, friendships and social interactions of his community. He does not show extreme discomfort with the kinds of sensory experiences that are ordinary for most people.

Level 2.0 Minimum/Trace

Slight traces of autism spectrum characteristics are seen at this Level. The observed behavioral and mental characteristics can be thought of as inconveniences or slight departures from normatively-prevalent behavior and cognition. At this Level the traits are not usually considered to be substantially handicapping. This zone of the autism spectrum occupies the space between Typical functioning on one hand, and the appearance of clearly identifiable autistic characteristics on the other.

Participant: Carmen

Domain 1. Social Relationships.

Carmen is interested in meeting other people and developing friendships. While often successful, her approach to social interactions is somewhat uncertain and awkward. Carmen is sometimes described as being "slightly out of synch" or "shy".

Carmen has some difficulty understanding some of the subtler points of social interaction. The problem areas may include her difficulty with understanding the implications of some facial expressions and also the speaker's tone of voice.

Participants at this Level are emotionally connected to other family members and demonstrate, through their behavior and expressions, that they value their place within the family. The families usually adjust to these persons' personal style, and when needed compensate for the child's areas of need. This adjustment is usually accomplished without special counseling or professional advice.

Domain 2. Language Expression.

The participant's development of language expression abilities is slightly behind those of other children in the same age group. Her ability to speak words, phrases and complex sentences are somewhat less skilled or a bit more uncertain than other children in her age-cohort.

When the participant was a young child she had not yet mastered standard English. Because of that she could creatively produce phrases and descriptions such as "My shirt is outside out" or "The shoe is upside up".

Despite these small delays in the development of language proficiency this participant maintained an active interest in communicating with other people, and thus supporting the social-interactive relationship. Even though some of her statements were imperfectly formed they were nonetheless usually understood and accepted by the listeners of the conversation.

Domain 3. Types of Interests.

The participant at this Level shows a slight preference for engaging in an individual activity, rather than reaching out for interaction with another person or seeking the attention of an audience. These participants are somewhat less interested than the Typical person in sampling a wide variety of activities and experiences. Some thoughtful planning and well-placed encouragement by her family and teachers can be beneficial in moving the participant at this Level to more skills and wider horizons.

Domain 4. Personal Management and Self-Direction.

The participant's goal-setting, activity-planning personal management skills are slightly less well developed than most people in her age group. There can be a lot of variability in the strengths and skill development that co-exist within her collection of personal management and self-direction abilities.

Carmen may need some reminders, suggestions, and short demonstrations in order to keep her schoolwork, clothing, and personal possessions in reasonably good order. While she might be quite good at remembering an array of new information, she might be less effective at deciding which of her activities needed the most effort and attention (setting priorities).

Although the participant's ability to review, evaluate, and self-correct are not so well developed as other in her age-groups, she is open to suggestions and guidance from her family, teachers, and mentors. As a result of that openness to guidance she is generally successful in completing her schoolwork, home chores, vocational assignments and recreational activities.

Domain 5. Language Understanding. Receptive Language.

Carmen understands the meaning of fewer words and word-combinations than her peers do. Her overall understanding of language is slightly below that of others in her peer group.

In order to understand the meaning of idioms or figures of speech like "A penny saved is a penny earned" or "Don't cry over spilled milk" Carmen may require some supplementary explanation which involve more examples of the idiom Participants at this Level may not always communicate an "I don't know" statement because they incorrectly assume knowledge of the word-combinations.

Participants like Carmen typically do not ignore the speaker, except in instances where that would be appropriate.

Domain 6. Social Use of Language. Pragmatic Language.

Carmen has some difficulty with adjusting the volume (loudness) of her voice. In conversation she may be too loud or too soft. She may have a somewhat flat voice that doesn't express much change in tone or in rate of speaking. It is not always clear whether she is enthusiastic about a topic or not.

She may unintentionally interrupt another speaker, or alternately may pause politely while the other person speaks, and then continues with her own sentence as though there were no other conversational partners. Carmen may appear awkward about starting conversations, especially around topics that are mostly social or personal.

Domain 7. Body Language. Nonverbal Communication.

Carmen is not quite so skilled as her age-peers at understanding or reading facial expressions, body language, or gestures. She might be somewhat uncertain in using her own facial expressions, body language or gestures to communicate her ideas, emotions and intentions.

She may prefer a reduced amount of eye contact during a conversation, often looking away from her conversational partner. Carmen is somewhat less skilled than her peers with easily adjusting the physical space between her and her conversation partner, occasionally under-or-over estimating that space.

Domain 8. Flexibility and Transitions.

The participant may prefer routines throughout the day. Established routines are the structure upon which she relies for getting through the day. Routines are the pathways for daily activities such as getting ready for school, preparing the table for dinner, getting ready for bed, etc.

Carmen may need to be coached about what to expect before beginning a new experience such as getting on an airplane, going to the beach, or changing to a different school. She feels comfortable when games have clearly-defined rules, and may seem a little lost with free-form play or activities that rely on imagination and fantasy.

This participant is more likely than the typical person to have difficulty changing her mind once she has decided on an opinion. Some people might describe her as "rigid" in her thinking.

Carmen can seem bothered or upset when asked to change activities. She may take extra time to finish with one activity before being willing to move on to the next one. These preferences for routine and constancy sometimes present inconveniences and challenges to the participant, her caregivers and her teachers. However, on the whole these preferences do not seriously disrupt the events of her daily life.

Domain 9. Repeating Body Movements. Movement Stereotypes.

Carmen is not quite so skillful with fine and large muscle activities as most people of her age. She is more likely than most of her age-peers to do some small repeating behaviors such as tapping her fingers or feet, pacing back and forth, or brushing her hair.

She developed a preference for either the right or left hand somewhat later than most children. Her handwriting, especially cursive, is less clear than the writing of other people in her age group. Carmen usually has some favorite object such as a wristwatch, pencil, decorative pin, necklace, bracelet or jacket button that she likes to hold and manipulate.

Carmen does not intentionally strike her head against hard objects, nor does she hit or bite herself. She does not produce other self-hurting behaviors (normal accidents are excluded).

Domain 10. Creative Imagination.

The participant may use small toys such as action figures, dolls, animals, or cars to tell a story. However, the story is likely to be a re-telling of one already known to her, rather than an example of a mostly original idea or script.

The participant is not drawn to activities that emphasize fantasy, vivid imagination or speculation, especially if they appear to have no useful purpose. She is unlikely to seek out make-believe games or role-playing dramas.

Carmen applies her creativity and imagination towards activities and projects that are practical, reasonable and possibly useful. She is not a dreamer, but rather a very down-to-earth and realistic person.

She prefers to do things whose outcomes can be anticipated and which are achievable, such as working on math problems, learning the lines of an already-written play, or drawing pictures that are clear and realistic.

Domain 11. Imitation and Empathy.

She can observe an action or series of actions and is then able to attempt an imitation or repetition of those actions. However, she might require more time and practice than the Typical participant in order to be successful. She is able to "put herself in someone else's shoes", but not so easily or as fully as the Typical participant of her age.

Carmen can understand how another person might think about or experience some event, but requires additional explanation and discussion in order to reach that understanding.

Domain 12. Unusual Sensory Events.

She is more sensitive than most people to some textures. She may dislike certain materials touching her skin such as velvet, burlap or wool. She may also dislike foods or liquids such as oatmeal, smoothies, carrots or other crunchy foods.

Carmen may have a negative reaction to certain sounds, and they may cause her to pull away. The unwanted sounds may annoy her the same way others might be bothered by the sound of fingernails on a chalkboard or a squeaky balloon.

She may be more than usually sensitive to certain smells. This participant does <u>not</u> replace friendships and social activity with sensory stimulation.

Level 3.0 Borderline

Autism spectrum traits that interfere with the child's functioning in one or more areas are seen. This zone of the autism spectrum had previously been identified with the category/diagnosis of Asperger Disorder. Constructive interventions in these areas (use of language, social interaction skills, personal organization, etc.) can produce important improvements. Even though there are definite recognizable areas of concern, on balance the individuals remain largely competent and functional. They can realistically be expected to be active and responsive participants in educational and vocational activities.

Participant: Juan

Domain 1. Social Relationships.

Among participants at this Level the need for social relationships is reduced, but it is not absent. Sometimes Juan would like to develop a friendship, but he usually just doesn't know how to do it very well. Juan usually gets along reasonably well with people who are either younger or older than he is, but not so well with his peers. People who are much older or younger than Juan are likely to be more accepting and less critical than people of the same age group. Juan is more likely to develop good friendships when the friends are especially accepting and flexible.

The participant often behaves and speaks in ways that are more formal and "stodgy" than is usual for people of his age. This style of speaking becomes an issue for starting and keeping friendships. Juan is less skillful than most people with the background unstated rules (conventions) of play, games, and social interaction. Because of this relative shortage of social skills, he is frequently not selected for friendships by his peers, and unfortunately may indeed be teased or avoided by them.

Domain 2. Language Expression.

The participant's abilities with language expression can span a wide range, from slightly below average too much below average. Juan's main challenge is in the ways in which he can use language as a method for carrying on a back-and-forth dialogue. For this Level the essential question is that of reciprocity. Can those who are speakers change roles and become listeners? Participants who are at Level 3.0 have more-than-average difficulty with the process of reciprocity. They are more likely to prefer the speakers' role than the listeners' role

Juan has a style of speaking that is more formal and measured than is usual for young people. For that reason, he and other Level 3.0 participants are sometimes described as "Little Professors". (This feature is covered more fully in Domain 4).

Domain 3. Types of Interests.

By the time Juan is 6 or 7 years old he has developed particularly strong interests, even expertise, in one or two specific subject areas.

Some illustrative examples are the dates of shipwrecks, reptiles, sports statistics, vocabulary definitions, transportation routes, the pattern of days-of-the-week on a calendar, and detailed computer and electronic equipment operations. The participant may also be very interested in taking objects apart, and most of the time he put them back together.

The young participant usually takes the initiative in the process of collecting information about the preferred subjects. Adults are useful as sources of information and materials when the young participant is unable to obtain them on his own. The participants at this Level place a great deal of importance on their favorite activities and interests. Participants like Juan are able to focus on these topics for longer spans of time (hyper focus) than the typical person. As a result of this heightened capacity for concentration they are able to learn some materials in greater depth and detail than most people usually achieve.

Juan does feel the need to check in, from time to time, with friends and family to share what he is doing, and to maintain his existing social contacts. However, the participant has less need for the attention of an audience than typical participants do, and he often selects activities that do not involve other people.

The participants at this Level can do well with activities such as swimming, bicycle riding, running, bowling, archery, golf, skating, and tennis.

Serious participation in team sports like basketball, baseball, football, soccer and hockey would be quite unusual.

Domain 4. Personal Management and Self-Direction.

The clash between the participant's personal management and self-direction abilities on one hand, versus the presence of disrupting characteristics on the other begin to be seen at this Level. The dominating aspect of the participant's personal management and self-direction capability is that of <u>selectivity</u>. He seems very skilled at some self-management strategies, and quite unskilled at others. Some portions of Juan's goal-setting and activity-management skills can be more highly developed than those of the typical participant. He often has the ability to choose a topic of interest and achieve an unusually high level of skill and competence in that topic.

The participant can very effectively filter-out or disregard competing or distracting background events. However, this heightened ability to focus his attention comes with some costs, such as a reduced ability to smoothly switch from one activity to another. He has a tendency to "stay on track", even when a change would be better for the immediate situation. Juan's approach to the arrangement of materials, personal possessions, and equipment for projects are likewise very selective. Those materials that fit into his areas of interest are quite well organized. Materials and objects that are outside the scope of his serious interests are often a jumble of disorganization.

The combination of high levels of competence, along with the participant's tendency to ignore or disregard surrounding events result in the stylistic label of "A young absent-minded professor". The participants at this Level bring a lot of skill and enthusiasm to their areas of interest, but they often have difficulty with generating an overview, with seeing or understanding "the big picture".

Domain 5. Language Understanding, Receptive Language.

The participant's understanding of common words, unusual words and word-combinations cover a wide range, varying from slightly below average too much above average. Juan's main difficulties have to do with idioms and figures of speech. These phrases are incorrectly comprehended as literal statements. Statements such as "All is lost", "That's water under the bridge", or "That dog won't hunt" are taken literally, and thus misinterpreted. They may not be understood at all.

Juan has difficulty understanding language-based jokes or humor that contains fine points of language. The participants at this Level are more likely than typical persons to not comprehend or to misinterpret the mood or the tone of a conversation.

Domain 6. Social Use of Language. Pragmatic Language.

The participant has some difficulty with using his word knowledge as a resource for relating to people. Teachers and caregivers may refer to him as "The Young Encyclopedia" because of his expertise in one or more subject areas. Supported by an active curiosity and a great memory, participants at this Level collect great stores of facts on their favorite topics, but are also relatively indifferent to areas in which they have less personal involvement.

When the participant speaks about a preferred topic his tone of voice and rate of speech may appear excited or rushed, as though he is trying to present a large amount of knowledge into one conversational turn. On the other hand, when he joins in a discussion whose topic was chosen by someone else, he might seem hesitant, shy, or speak in a monotone (a flat voice).

The participant is not a very good listener. When he is involved in a conversation he usually talks at the person, rather than with them. He is capable of recognizing and understanding the meaning of what the other people have to say, but he is not very interested in encouraging them to fully express their point of view or knowledge.

Juan and his Same-Level participants may very well be kind-hearted and caring people, but they are poor judges of how their statements are being received. They can – and do – say things to people that seem annoying, upsetting, insensitive, or inappropriate. When this happens the participants are often surprised or puzzled by the reaction of the conversational partner. It was not their intention to upset anyone.

Domain 7. Body Language. Nonverbal Communication.

The participant often misinterprets body language and gestures, or seems not to notice them at all. For example, he might not distinguish between an expression of concern, versus an expression of fear. Likewise, he might miss the difference between a brief grin and a broad smile. The participant's own use of facial expressions, body language and gestures are considerably less skilled than others in his age group.

Juan's natural tendency is to produce fleeting eye contact, rather than the more relaxed ongoing gaze that takes place in ordinary conversation. When he is reminded about this feature he can usually improve his eye-contact, at least temporarily.

The participant is not very good at judging the proper distance between himself and his conversation partners. He may stand too close, or he may select an awkwardly wide distance between them. In either instance his personal distance is not culturally appropriate, at least at first, before suggestions for correction are accepted.

Domain 8. Flexibility and Transitions.

Juan expresses a preference for games that have clearly-defined rules. He usually does not ask to be included in creative, free-form play with other people and other people usually do not invite him to join them. The participant may show a lack of flexibility in his thinking or problem-solving skills. He is reluctant to change an idea or concept that he has accepted as correct, even when new information is introduced. For this reason, misunderstandings are hard to change, and often seem "set in stone.

Juan is bothered or upset when suddenly asked to change activities, and may even have tantrums. He often appreciates a five-minute warning before being asked to transition from one activity to the next. The participant's lack of flexibility and difficulty with transitions sometimes presents challenges to family members and friends, who are asked to be especially patient, considerate, and creative in dealing with these characteristics.

Domain 9. Repeating Body Movements. Movement Stereotypes.

As noted in the previous section if the participant's difficulties with body movements and gestures are the result of cerebral palsy or neurological injury, the understanding of this section should be modified and interpreted with considerable caution.

Juan had, and may still have some difficulty with large-muscle coordination and balance. He had challenges with learning to do things like ride a bicycle, skate, catch a ball or walk a balance beam. He also had difficulty with fine-muscle coordination and was less skillful than others in his age group with activities like fastening buttons, working zippers, picking up small marbles or handling a deck of playing cards.

When this participant is excited or stressed he may flap or wring his hands, rock back and forth, or pinch his clothing. These repeating body movements usually do <u>not</u> happen every day. He may also produce unusual facial grimaces or tics, but these also do not happen every day.

The participant does not intentionally strike his head against hard objects, nor does he hit or bite himself. He does not produce other self-hurting behaviors (normal accidents not included.)

Domain 10. Creative Imagination.

Juan is more likely than his peers to prefer independent or solo imaginative play. He is able to use action figures, dolls, and toys for his own make-believe play in much the same way as the typical child. However, he encounters difficulty with <u>shared</u> imaginative play.

On those occasions in which cooperative or shared imaginative play is attempted with other children the story-line does not fit well. His playmates are often puzzled or confused by the way in which his story-line doesn't build on or connect to the story-line produced by the other children.

The participant limits his make-believe games and creativity to one or two preferred subjects, and has difficulty creating other story-lines. He is usually more interested in the practical ways in which an object works, than he is in the appearance of the object or the way this object fits into its surroundings.

Juan has some difficulty imagining what another person's point of view might be.

Domain 11. Imitation and Empathy.

The participant can imitate or copy most of the straightforward, uncomplicated actions and language that he observes. However, he is less skillful in using imitation to learn the fine points and subtle variations of social interaction, styles of speaking and polite behavior. He may not recognize that a situation requires a different approach, a new alternative, or an exception to the usual rule.

Juan has some difficulty with "putting himself into someone else's shoes". For example, when he is talking with someone he may be unaware that the other person wishes to speak, or that a listener might be bored or annoyed with him.

Domain 12. Unusual Sensory Events.

The participant can be very particular and demanding about sensory experiences and materials. He may remove all the tags and labels from his shirts because the slight thickness bothers him. He may insist on wearing socks inside-out or prefer to wear no socks at all. He may avoid certain materials such as denim, velvet or wool. He may prefer very loose-fitting clothing. Juan may also have strong dislikes in food textures as well as some odors.

He may prefer certain types of lighting. He may complain of headaches at school and need to wear a baseball cap or sunglasses in rooms that have fluorescent lighting. He may even dislike the distinctive buzzing sound produced by those fluorescent lights.

This participant does not usually replace friendships and social interactions with simple sensory stimulation. However, he may have a strong interest in filling large portions of his time with complicated sensory stimulation such as video games.

If Juan has an interest in or talent for music, he might practice or play music for long spans of time.

Level 4.0 Mild

Clear and distinctive traits of autism that are significantly handicapping are seen in all or nearly all areas of behavior, thinking, and social-educational functioning. While the autism-spectrum behaviors and traits are real and challenging, the child still retains the capacity for meaningful participation in many of the social, educational, and vocational activities of daily life. The milder zones of this Level are known as "high-functioning autism". A wide range of interventions and supports are needed.

Participant: Raven

Domain 1. Social Relationships.

The participant has a definite preference for activities that do not involve interaction with other people. She has very few, if any friends outside of the family, and she is usually not bothered by this situation. When Raven is away from her immediate family she prefers that social interactions be very brief and very limited. She was not a "cuddly" baby or toddler, and did not snuggle. She usually had very little interest in being touched, and she rarely gazed directly into the eyes of nearby people.

Raven will begin an interaction with a family member when she needs something specific, such as food, beverage, access to video games, DVD's, music, computers, or a favorite object. Otherwise she prefers to be left alone.

The participants who are at this Level care about and are emotionally connected to their parents and siblings, and clearly recognize that their parents are important for their well-being and comfort, and further that the parents are the providers of shelter, comfort, guidance, food and protection.

However, the ways in which Raven expresses those feelings of caring and connection are much subtler and restrained than those of typical children. For example, she might twirl the parent's hair around her fingers in a matter-of-fact way, or place herself near the parent's lap and accept hugs and expressions of affection without returning the feeling or gesture.

Domain 2. Language Expression.

Raven showed a significant delay in the development of speech and language. Either she did not speak in sentences by the time she was three years old, or she was developing language in a normal way and then lost some or all of that skill. A hearing loss may have been suspected.

The participant has definite problems with engaging in a back-and-forth conversation as a result of those difficulties with spoken language. While her ability to engage in conversation is greatly reduced (when compared to Typical development, it is not completely absent. Raven can and does produce meaningful conversations. However, her sentences tend to be brief and limited.

The participants at this Level may show as many as 4 of the following 6 language-and-communication issues:

1. Sometimes replaces the word "I" with the word "he" "she" or "you."
2. Invents their own words. A flashlight might be called a "light stick", while roller skates could be named "roll shoe".
3. Produces a variety of sounds that are not standard words. Speaks in jargon.
4. Echo or "parrot" words a phrases. This activity is named echolalia.
5. Sentences are spoken in a flat tone, or with an unusual rhythm.
6. The participants prefer to not initiate (start) a conversation with another person.

Domain 3. Types of Interests.

Raven has little interest in sampling and learning from a wide variety of experiences. When the participant becomes involved in a subject or activity, she is focused mostly on the way the activity feels, rather than on how the audience will react to what she is doing. The participant might become very interested in a specific object and then take it apart. However, she has little interest in putting it back together.

Raven shows an on-and-off pattern of attention to what is going on around her. She can be aware of and involved with the surrounding activities for a short span of time. When that span is over she returns to her unshared thoughts, repeating movements, or fascination with some sensory stimulation such as a pattern of lights, the sound of her own voice, or the texture of her clothing.

The participant rarely seeks praise or approval for her accomplishments from those around her. It is also very unusual for her to actively share her activities and interests with other people. Despite this apparent indifference, the participants at this Level can be comforted and reassured by the praise and approval they receive from caregivers, teachers, and mentors.

When praise and approval are offered they can help the participants behave in a calm and constructive way. The participant's difficulties with anticipating or recognizing the consequences of an unsafe activity set boundaries on what she is able to do. The kinds of recreational and sports activities in which Raven can safely participate need to be arranged, organized, and supervised by responsible adults more closely and for a longer span of time than is done for the typical person.

Some participants like Raven express an interest in developing skill in playing a musical instrument. The instrument can be played either in a solo performance, or in association with one or more other musicians. Playing a musical instrument offers a range of choices about the degree of relational directness in which the musician wishes to engage.

Domain 4. Personal Management and Self-Direction.

The clash between the personal management self-direction resources *versus* the participant's disruptive developmental features increases in intensity at this Level. Raven's difficulty with imagination, combined with a limited tolerance for change have the effect of shrinking her ability to generate and develop an adequate inventory of problem-solving strategies. It is very difficult for her to identify useful alternatives when she has considerable difficulty generating or welcoming new possibilities.

The participant does have a strong interest in arranging objects and activities, as seen in her tendency to arrange personal objects into a specific pattern, as well as a clearly expressed preference for very predictable schedules. (This preference may be expressed behaviorally rather than vocally.) However, problems develop when objects and materials need to be reorganized in and creative ways.

The participant is not able to effectively rearrange her possessions, schedules, or activities on a regular basis, without outside help. Her considerable preference for predictable, consistent routines do not fit in very well with the requirements of the personal management/self-direction operations of flexible attention and the ability to review a variety of alternatives.

It is very difficult for Raven to see "the big picture", the overview. Her natural way of operating is to focus on objects, events, or activities that are specific, real, touchable and capable of being directly experienced. Moving to an abstract overview is both difficult and unlikely.

Raven and her Same-Level peers are able to cooperate in developing the plans or series of steps for managing their work, but are (usually) unable to independently create multi-step agendas.

Domain 5. Language Understanding. Receptive Language.

Raven's understanding of language varies from slightly below average to considerably below average. It is sometimes difficult to know if she understands the meaning of specific words because she often does not react to the speaker's statement.

When Raven and her Same-Level peers were younger than three years old they appeared to not hear sounds. A hearing loss was suspected, and in most cases that problem was put aside after an examination.

Raven remains selective about the words and sounds to which she will react. It is not unusual for the participant to look away when her name is spoken to her, or she simply does not respond.

Domain 6. Social Use of Language. Pragmatic Language.

This participant is not interested in conversing about topics other than those of her own choosing. She may ignore attempts to engage her in these conversations, or she may wait for an opening and then abruptly switch to the topic she prefers.

Raven's ability and interest in engaging in a balanced back-and-forth conversation is very limited. When given a choice about speaking she usually prefers to say as little as will allow her to "get by". At other times she might remain silent or simply walk away without giving any explanation for her behavior. These behaviors become especially relevant and influential during adolescence, a time when young people are increasing their social contacts among their peers.

With a great deal of effort, the participant may learn "scripts" which provide the basis or framework for participating in a conversation. This approach is useful for brief conversations, but is rarely able to support conversations that are extensive or detailed.

Raven may not understand nor remember the basic rules of conversation. She may interrupt others, speak over them, or raise her volume (loudness) above the other speaker's voice. If she pauses when another person speaks, an observer may get the idea that she is not listening with interest, but rather is planning what she will say while she is waiting for her turn to talk.

Domain 7. Body Language. Nonverbal Communication.

As noted in the previous section, if the participant's difficulties with body movements and gestures are the result of cerebral palsy or neurological injury, the understanding of this section should be modified and interpreted with considerable caution.

The participant at this Level does not know how to receive messages and information from the body language, facial expressions, and gestures produced by other people. Raven does not intentionally use her own body language to communicate with others. She avoided looking directly into someone else's eyes even before she was five years old, and this preference continues to the present day. There is very little eye contact and she rarely holds a typical gaze with another person.

Raven may give some attention to a speaker by turning (orienting) her body in the speaker's direction, but at the same time decline to look directly at the speaker's face.

Basic Concept: The participant's reluctance (or inability) to communicate through body language and gestures is basically another aspect of her consistent orientation to minimize communications and interactions with the people in her living-space.

Domain 8. Flexibility and Transitions.

Raven places a definite emphasis on a known routine and a predictable schedule. Her ability to transition between activities benefits greatly from consistent practice and rehearsal of that transition schedule.

Her constructive cooperative behavior is shaped by rules that were learned with considerable effort by her, and taught with considerable effort by her caregivers, teachers, and other family members. It is very difficult for Raven to understand that these rules can be modified, and indeed that it may sometimes be necessary to make those changes. The participant may be bothered by what would ordinarily be small changes in her home environment, such as a new picture on the wall or the rearrangement of furniture. Raven directs her attention to a specific, sharply-focused activity, and is very reluctant to leave that activity and move on to another.

Parents and caregivers have learned to adapt their schedules and daily activities to meet the participant's need for constancy and routine. Her need for constancy may be evident in the way she resists changes in the day's schedule. She may react poorly to changes in the time at which dinner is eaten, or the time set aside for TV viewing.

As suggested above, she has noticeable difficulty with making transitions from one situation or event to another. She usually requires more than a five-minute advance notice in order to cooperate with a previously unplanned transition. She may require more advance notice, some additional reminders, or the offer of a reward.

**Domain 9. Repeating Body Movements.
Movement Stereotypes.**

As noted in an earlier section if the participant's difficulties with body movements and gestures are the result of cerebral palsy or neurological injury, the understanding of this section should be modified and interpreted with considerable caution.

At this Level the participant produces one or more of the unusual repeating movements listed below, which typically happen every day. Some of the behaviors may happen several times each day. The behaviors are:

1.   Walking on tip-toes
2.   Whirling or turning in a circle
3.   Flapping of the hands.
4.   Rocking back-and-forth, either while sitting or standing.
5.   Wiggling or flicking the fingers
6.   Slapping the side of the body. Open hand, non-injurious.

These repetitive movements may briefly interrupt Raven's activities, and distract others who are around her. However, these unusual behaviors are not so frequent or so severe that they seriously disrupt the continuity of her activities or schedule.

Raven does not intentionally strike her head against hard objects, nor does she hit or bite herself. She does not produce other self-hurting behaviors (normal accidents are excluded).

Domain 10. Creative Imagination.

Raven can name or identify her various toys or action figures (cowboy, police officer, fire-fighter, dancer, magician, dollhouse, baby, princess, everyday people, etc.) but she does not create any stories or make-believe dramas with them. She is interested in the physical appearance of her toys, such as their shape, color, size, or texture. These toys are arranged, lined up or stacked in a specific way, often on the basis of these physical features.
This participant did not develop imaginative play and make-believe stories, or these were expressed in a very limited way. The use of imagination involves only a very small part of her daily life. She goes through her day based mostly on what has been well learned, and on what can be clearly seen, heard, touched or tasted.

She has little or no interest in speculation, conjecture, or in trying to imagine possibilities that she has not already experienced. Visual aids are useful when discussing abstract concepts. For example, a discussion of "next week" or "next month" would benefit from a calendar so that these participants can see the number of days that are involved.

Domain 11. Imitation and Empathy.

Raven's ability to imitate and copy behavior is significantly under-developed. She learns basic social conduct and conventions more slowly and with more effort than her typical peers. The ability to imitate spoken sounds and words is significantly decreased, resulting in large delays in the development of speech and language. She has only a very basic (i.e., limited) ability to intuitively recognize and understand someone else's intentions or feelings.

Given very purposeful, concentrated instruction Raven can identify major conditions that produce happiness or sadness, satisfaction or disappointment, safety or danger. However, she is usually not interested in recognizing the subtler or shaded emotional states in other people. She usually does not understand that another person feels embarrassed, annoyed, disappointed or anxious.

Domain 12. Unusual Sensory Events.

Raven's involvement with sensory stimulation is quite inconsistent. She expresses an attraction to some kinds of sensory stimulation, but also shows an aversion to other types. She may be fascinated by patterns of flickering lights and may produce a similar sensation by flicking or flapping her fingers in front of her eyes. She may appear to not hear some ordinary sounds and later may cover her ears in an attempt to block out a slightly different sound.

She can focus on or become immersed in the experience of simple sensory stimulation. The sensory input can come from a variety of sources, including the sensation of water from a faucet flowing over her hands, the sensation of muscle movements while rocking back and forth, the experience of the textures of various kinds of cloths, and patterns of light or music.

If left to her own preferences this participant will allow sensory stimulation to replace friendships, social interaction, and shared activities.

Level 5.0 Moderate

Clear and distinctive traits of autism which are significantly handicapping and which result in definite impairment are seen in all or nearly all areas of behavior, thinking, and social-educational functioning. These behavioral and mental characteristics have a strong impact on the child's environment, including the physical aspects of his/her residence, the quality of personal relationships, the demands on caregivers, and the teaching skills of educators. Extensive interventions and supports are required.

Participant: Dustin

Domain 1. Social Relationships.

This participant is very selective about interactions with people. It is not unusual for him to reject or ignore another person's efforts to interact or communicate with him. He can become exhausted or upset when urged to interact with other people. If the request for interaction is too intense or stressful he may become upset, agitated or otherwise misbehave in order to avoid the interaction.

Dustin has little or no flexibility regarding the norms of appropriate behavior, which he has learned with considerable effort. He consistently applies these rules or guidelines to specific situations, and continues to apply them even if the context or circumstances change.

He may cooperate briefly when another person makes a request about completing a chore or a school assignment. Then, when left to his own preferences he returns to solitary activity. In the classroom his reaction to the teacher's instructions can be very limited.

Dustin often does not acknowledge the presence of other people, and in fact can behave as if they are not there. For example, he might ignore a request to pass a dish at dinner.

As with Level 4.0 these participants were not "cuddly" babies and did not snuggle. They prefer not to be touched and resist gazing into the eyes of other people.

Dustin and others at this Level rarely show affection openly. They usually do not spontaneously offer hugs, kisses, or gestures of warmth. However, being at home in the presence of their family prompts a sense of safety and relative calm. The participants are much more likely to cooperate with members of the family than with newly-introduced people, because family members have the advantage of being familiar, known and therefore trusted.

Domain 2. Language Expression.

The production of spoken language is very difficult for Dustin. When sentences are spoken the statements tend to be no longer than three or four words. Dustin can become fascinated with a specific topic or subject, and repeat brief phrases or questions many times. However, the brief phrases or questions are spoken as a matter of intense personal fascination, rather than a mode of communication. Dustin and other participants whose expressive language skills are at Level 5.0 can also show any of the six spoken language variations that are specified (above) in Level 4.0. However, overall speech production is more limited than is seen in Level 4.0.

Dustin may feel more comfortable communicating ideas and requests through the use of various assisted communication devices. These devises include write-boards, picture selection, laptop computers, and electronic digital tablets. For some ASD people the use of American Sign Language is a helpful alternative to communicating by voicing. Elementary skills with American Sign Language can be exercised by children as young as five years of age.

Domain 3. Types of Interests.

The participant has almost no interest in exploring the broad range of activities that most people enjoy. All or almost all of the participant's interests are concentrated on very specific activities, or on objects that they can touch, move, arrange or otherwise directly experience. Most of these activities can be done in a few steps, usually no more than two or three.

A brief inventory of appropriate recreational activities for participants at this Level may include recreational walking or swimming (with careful supervision), listening to music, viewing a dramatic video, striking a ball with a bat (as in T ball), and finger painting. Very few of the participant's activities are shared with another person. Dustin may accept another person's participation in the activities, but usually does not request it.

The participant usually has little concern for the presence or reactions of an audience, whether that audience is large or small. The participants may, from time to time, briefly inspect their surroundings, usually to assure themselves that all is well, and that no sudden changes have been introduced to their routine or living-space.

Domain 4. Personal Management and Self-Direction.

The participant's developmental features that are disruptive have taken over his personal management and self-direction functions, such as his ability to screen out distractions and unimportant background events. Dustin's screening-out function has grown out of proportion, throwing his personal management abilities out of balance. The screening-out function has overwhelmed the other abilities, pushing them aside. As a result, Dustin has great difficulty in adjusting or regulating his actions and thinking.

Most of Dustin's attention is focused on some preferred object, movement, pattern of lights or sounds, repeating phrases or behavioral ritual. He usually ignores some useful choices that would allow him to deal with his surroundings more effectively, and thus increase his well-being. At this Level of behavior (Level 5.0) Dustin is typically not resourceful or flexible enough to generate a "to-do" list of varied activities without significant input and guidance from other people, nor would he effectively accomplish the tasks on that list without specific assistance and guidance from those mentors.

Domain 5. Language Understand. Receptive Language.

The participant's understanding of language and receptiveness to spoken language is very limited. He is sometimes able to cooperate when a trusted person makes a simple, direct request for a specific action. As with Level 4.0 a hearing loss was suspected and in most cases that problem was put aside after an examination.

The participants have little or no understanding of idioms or figures of speech such as "Hop to it", "Break the bank", or "Step up to the plate", and do not achieve long-lasting comprehension even after an explanation. Dustin reacts to the speaker's statements or questions very hesitantly, and may need several repetitions of the statement in order to reply.

Domain 6. Social Use of Language. Pragmatic Language.

This participant may speak in a monotone and thus sound "flat", or he may be inappropriately loud or excited. When Dustin speaks it appears to take a lot of effort, and his speech patterns are very different from those of the age-peers whose development is typical.

Dustin does not like to wait his turn, preferring instead to make his statements without regard to the readiness of the listener or the audience. This participant can be blunt and thus appear rude. Dustin may answer direct questions, but have great difficulty with including another person's statement into his own conversational turn. He is not interested in what other people have to say.

The speech of these participants may be sprinkled with sudden changes in the topic, unrelated to the stream of conversation (known as *non sequiturs*). Other people in their age group do not enjoy speaking with them.

Domain 7. Body Language. Nonverbal Communication.

This participant has extreme difficulty understanding facial expressions, body language or gestures. This difficulty continues even when he is provided with coaching, reminders, and hints. He is unable to produce a relevant integrated reaction when he is given the combination of spoken statements and gestured communication. He may even ignore a body language message as straightforward as someone pointing toward a specific object while saying "Look over there".

Dustin does not seem able to intentionally pretend, act, or model an emotion by using body language, facial expressions, or gestures. As a result of these limitations a participant who is nine years old or older does not use or understand the style of sarcasm because facial expressions and gestures play a part in the combination of criticism and humor that convey sarcasm.

Although the participant does not intentionally communicate non-verbally, he may produce a range of body movements, gestures and facial expressions that express his emotional state. The responsibility for "reading" these patterns rest with the participant's caregiver and other observers.

Dustin prefers a personal space that is much wider than is typical, and the dimensions of this personal space remain fairly constant.

Domain 8. Flexibility and Transitions.

Dustin is deeply attached to his daily routines, behavior rituals and repetitions. He does not cope well when his routine is changed. When things do not happen in the expected order he is likely to become angry or agitated. He may temporarily refuse to cooperate or he may engage in self-hurting behaviors.

The participant shows great inflexibility in thinking and problem-solving. He depends on sameness in most aspects of his life – the same foods, the same desk, the same schedule, the same activities. Major changes in the participant's life, such as changes in his classroom, school, neighborhood, doctor or family vacation plans often result in major "meltdowns". Parents, caregivers and teachers need to do considerable pre-teaching in order to reduce such incidents.

Domain 9. Repeating Body Movements. Movement Stereotypes.

If the participant's difficulties with body language, gestures, and facial expressions are the result of cerebral palsy or other neurological injury, the understanding of this Domain needs to be modified, and interpreted with considerable caution.

Dustin produces two or more kinds of the unusual repeating movements listed below. He may engage in these movements 6 to 9 times each day. As previously listed in Level 4.0 the behaviors are:

1. Walking on tip-toes
2. Whirling or turning in a circle
3. Flapping of the hands
4. Rocking back-and-forth, either while sitting or standing
5. Wiggling or flicking the fingers.
6. Slapping the side of the body.

These repetitive movements are frequent and severe enough to significantly interrupt the continuity of his activities and schedule. While these movements may convey tension, discomfort, anxiety, annoyance or anger, they are not the usual kinds of gestures and facial expressions with which most people communicate.

The participant might engage in serious self-hurting behaviors such as hitting himself or intentionally striking his head. These behaviors might happen 1 or 2 times per week, and can result in serious bodily injury.

Domain 10. Creative Imagination.

Dustin has some difficulty with naming or identifying his various toys or action figures. He does not use these playthings to express a story line or an imaginative drama. He is interested in the physical appearance of his toys and possessions, such as their shape, color, size or texture. He arranges, lines up or stacks these possessions on the basis of these physical features.

This participant did not develop imaginative play or make-believe stories. He does not participate in imaginative games or make-believe dramas with other children, and has no interest in doing so. His thinking and behavior are directed towards the physical objects that are immediately in front of him.

Dustin is not able to use imagination as a resource for creativity, constructive planning or relaxation. He has very strong preferences for a known and predictable routine. He needs and develops behavioral rituals that go far beyond the kinds of routine activities that are valued by most people.

Domain 11. Imitation and Empathy.

Dustin's ability to imitate and copy behavior is under-developed in major ways. He learns basic social conduct and conventions much more slowly and considerably less completely than typical participants. His ability to imitate spoken sounds and the words that are built from these sounds is dramatically lessened, resulting in widespread impairment in his ability to acquire speech and language.

Dustin's capacity to intuitively recognize and understand someone else's intentions and feelings is present in only a very fragmentary form. He is mostly focused on his own thoughts, movements and personal involvements. He has little to no interest in another person's emotions or thoughts.

Domain 12. Unusual Sensory Events.

At this Level Dustin's attraction to and rejection of certain forms of sensory stimulation is sharply divided. He seeks out a great deal of sensory stimulation that does not involve relating to people or participating in shared activities. He will also avoid or energetically reject other kinds of sensory experiences.

Dustin and his Same-Level peers seek out a wide variety of sensory stimulation, which may include any of those listed below.

1. Carrying a favorite object.
2. Spinning an object and staring at it.

3.   Sniffing or smelling objects.
4.   Tasting or licking objects that are not food.
5.   Flicking or flapping fingers in front of the eyes.
6.   Staring at changing patterns of lights.
7.   Stimulation by body movements, such as rocking back-and-forth.
8.   The stimulation that comes from hitting oneself.
9.   Repeating words and phrases over and over.
10. Producing sounds that are not standard words.
11. Rubbing the hands over some kind of texture such as carpets, terrycloth, silk or smooth hard surfaces.

There can be as many as 12 episodes a day for any of these behaviors.

Dustin also strongly rejects certain stimuli, including physical contact with other people. He does not like to be touched or held by another person. He might cover his ears with his hands in an effort to shut out certain sounds.

The participant rejects a wide range of food choices, settling on a very narrow menu. He might have no reaction at all to small cuts or bruises. This pattern of sensory fascination and rejection presents major obstacles to social relationships, participation in ordinary activities and the constructive experience of education.

Level 6.0 Severe

All of the areas of daily living activities are seriously impaired, and extensive interventions, supports, and specialized programming are required. The individuals' behavioral and mental characteristics have a large and nearly constant stressful impact on their environment. These impacts include concern for physical security at home, high levels of stressful demands on caregivers, and requirements for detailed instructions for nearly all of the array of independent living skills. Specialized education programs are appropriate.

Participant: Susana

Domain 1. Social Relationships.

The participant does not seek out friends and very rarely reacts or replies to gestures of friendship. Almost all offers of social interactions are rejected.

With steady consistent training at school she can be taught to cooperate with basic activities such as following a group leader to a specific location like a dining area, classroom, recreation area or bus stop. Susana generally does not show a reaction when a caregiver enters or leaves a room. Her observed behavior appears unattached and unconnected. The participants at this Level may allow a few family members to manage their care.

Domain 2. Language Expression.

If spoken language emerged at all after the age of 3, it was extremely limited and incomplete. The number of words that the participant uses are very considerably below average.

If the participant uses spoken language at all it is not for the purpose of promoting social contact or friendly personal interaction. Rather, the small amount of language is used to request valued materials or conditions, such as food, beverages, access to videos, computer games, music, etc. In the absence of spoken language Susana might use gestures and hands-on guidance to obtain those needed materials.

Domain 3. Types of Interests.

Susana has a strong preference for activities that are solitary and focused on objects, whenever she has the opportunity to do so. She has little or no interest in the reactions of an audience. The participant does not play games that involve two or more people, and has hardly any understanding or interest in the rules that describe those games.

The participants have little or no interest in activities or topics in which knowledge and useful skill can be increased steadily over a long span of time. The interests of participants at this Level are focused on repeated body movements, sensory stimulation such as a pattern of lights, the sound of their voice, the texture of their clothing, or a limited number of repeated activities.

Domain 4. Personal Management and Self-Direction.

The extent of the participant's developmental difficulties has thrown her personal management and self-direction functions even further out of balance. As a result, almost all of the essential personal management operations need to be put in place by a resource person. The participant is then given the responsibility of carrying out the plan and accomplishing the goals. The process involves ongoing corrections and suggestions for improvements.

Susana and her Same-Level peers can still be active participants in the process of developing plans for the daily routine and school activities, in the sense that they are capable of offering some form of approval or disapproval about aspects of the plan. Their feedback is more likely expressed through behavior than through words.

Susana shows the characteristic of a very limiting "tunnel vision". She prefers to focus all, or almost all of her attention on some favorite objects, repeating movements, pattern of light, pattern of sound, repeated phrases or behavioral rituals. The ability to review, track, evaluate, and self-correct her behavior is just about absent.

Domain 5. Language Understanding. Receptive Language.

The participant is severely limited in both the understanding of words, and in making meaningful reactions to other people's spoken language. She offers very little attention to other people's statements or questions.

Susana and her Same-Level peers show little or no understanding of complicated sentences. They also show essentially no understanding of figures of speech or idioms such as "Keep your eye on the ball" or "The early bird gets the worm".

The participant's reactions or replies to people's statements are so limited that it is very difficult to identify the difference between what she doesn't know versus what she is simply ignoring. When Susana was younger than three years old she appeared to not hear sounds. A hearing loss was suspected, and in most cases that issue was put aside after an examination.

Susana and other participants at this Level do not always act in response to spoken words and requests alone. The speaker may need to use hands-on guidance and prompts (such as demonstrations and modeling) in order to successfully complete the action.

Susana only cooperates with or appropriately reacts to a very small number of very familiar and trusted people, usually no more than three or four.

Domain 6. Social Use of Language. Pragmatic Language.

Susana and her Same-Level peers may avoid using speech to communicate their intentions and ideas, instead relying on physical prompts and cues, such as leading someone by the hand or guiding the person's hand toward the desired object.

Susana and her equal-ability peers may very briefly answer direct questions, but in a manner quite different from other (typical) people of their age. The reply may vary from a short one-word answer (the bare facts) to an emphatic rejection of the other person's (the speaker) attempts to hold a conversation with them.

Susana is unlikely to engage in conversation with other people.

Domain 7. Body Language. Nonverbal Communication.

The participant is unaware of or ignores most of the body language, facial expression, and gestures produced by others. To the extent that spoken language is understood, Susana is more likely to respond to brief, clear, straightforward spoken statements. She can also respond positively to nonverbal communications that involve direct, physical, hands-on guidance, demonstrations, and instructions.

The participant does not use nonverbal communications to express intentions, ideas, or needs, beyond what is seen in basically automatic reactions such as discomfort, anger, fright, laughter, fascination, or rejection of something.

Susana and her equally-capable peers prefer to have a lot of space between themselves and another person, and they consistently avoid eye contact, turning away when another person looks directly at them.

Domain 8. Flexibility and Transitions.

She has developed a complex and extensive set of personal routines and rules. These rules are used to organize and govern most, if not all aspects of her daily life. Susana insists on doing the same thing in the same way each time.

She requires of her day that each activity and each transition be identified so that she can anticipate and plan for the change. Susana may refuse to transition from a familiar activity to an unexpected "off-schedule" one. Her distress may result in a tantrum.

Changes in the way things are done, alterations in the order of daily events, or even changes in the arrangement of the furniture can – and do – cause emotional outbursts or other intense negative reactions.

Domain 9. Repeating Body Movements.
Movement Stereotypes.

She produces three or more types of the unusual, repeating movements listed below, as often as 10 to 15 times per day. These incidents are widespread and ongoing. As previously stated, the behaviors are:

1. Walking on tip-toes
2. Whirling or turning in a circle
3. Flapping of the hands
4. Rocking back-and-forth, either while sitting or standing
5. Wiggling or flicking the fingers
6. Slapping the side of the body.

These repetitive movements are intense and severe enough to seriously disrupt and interfere with Susana's activities and schedule. In some cases, the frequency and intensity of the participant's self-hurting behaviors can make it necessary to use protective clothing and accessories, such as gloves and protective headgear.

Domain 10. Creative Imagination.

Susana may arrange, collect, or stack objects based on physical features such as size, color, shape or texture. She did not develop any solo imaginative play, does not engage in any cooperative imaginative play, and shows no interest in doing so. The development and expression of imaginative ideas or creative thinking are not part of her daily activities.

She is deeply committed to her daily routines and behavior rituals, and can become very upset and agitated if these routines are changed in any way. The participant's highly ritualized behaviors are minimally connected to or influenced by other people. The rituals are not intended to be useful to her family, school, or community.

For this participant and others at the same Level the absence of imagination and the creative problem-solving abilities which imagination promotes make it extremely difficult – if not impossible – for them to deal effectively with new and possibly unsafe situations.

Domain 11. Imitation and Empathy.

The participant's ability to imitate and copy behavior is drastically under-developed to the point of being almost entirely absent. She learns basic social conduct and conventions very slowly and very incompletely. . Her ability to imitate spoken sounds and the words that are built from these sounds is severely under – developed to the point where there is little or no clearly spoken language. Her ability to imitate spoken sounds and the words that are built from these sounds is severely under – developed to the point where there is little or no clearly spoken language.

Susana requires ongoing steady guidance, support, and instruction in order to progress through a daily schedule. Her capacity to intuitively recognize and understand someone else's intentions, feelings, or desires is either completely absent or present in only a minimal way. She concentrates her attention on her own thoughts, feelings, sensations and movements. She has essentially no interest in another person's experiences or wishes.

Domain 12. Unusual Sensory Events.

Susana's sensory fascinations and rejections are intense and forceful. She seeks out a wide variety of sensory stimulations which may include – but are not limited to – the collection of methods that are listed previously in Level 5.0. There can be as many as 16 episodes a day for any of these behaviors.

Susana rejects many forms of sensory stimulation. The rejection is often forceful and sometimes aggressive. She rejects physical contact, eye contact, some food textures and can also reject some textures in clothing and furnishings.

The participant may refuse to walk barefoot, finger paint or wear clothing of specific materials. She may gag at certain odors and may have extremely sensitive hearing or vision issues, especially about fluorescent lights. She may insist on wearing sunglasses.

The combination of intense fascination and aggressive avoidance the participant shows for certain sensory stimuli present large obstacles for her. These energetic reactions make it even more difficult for her to form friendly interactive relationships, acquire skills and knowledge through education, and participate meaningfully in her community.

Level 7.0 Very Severe

All of the areas of behavior, use of language, activities of daily living, social relationships, education and vocational placement are very seriously impaired. Extensive interventions, supports and specialized programming are required. These include condition – relevant education, behavioral interventions, family support and respite, supported living arrangements when needed, and specialized vocational or day-activity programs for age-suitable individuals. Ongoing close supervision is recommended. The individuals' behavioral and mental characteristics can – and usually do – have a quite large and nearly constant impact on their environment and the people within it. Their needs for remediation are deep and extensive.

Participant: Scott

Domain 1. Social Relationships.

Scott completely rejects and avoids all back-and-forth social interaction. He appears to have no interest at all in friendships, social relations, conversations or pleasantly shared activities (such as table-top games, card-playing, tossing a ball back-and-forth, dancing). If left to his own preferences all of his activities would be solitary.

Scott is not attached to any caregivers or other family members. He reacts to family members in the same way that he reacts to strangers. Scott and other participants at this Level appear to be stuck in their own world.

Domain 2. Language Expression.

At this Level the language expression skills are extremely below average. Scott and other participants at this Level rarely or never express standard spoken language. If the participant uses language at all it is limited to no more than 4 or 5 words or short phrases per day. These sparse expressions are most likely used to communicate wants, needs, or feelings of discomfort. Scott is likely to use gestures or hands-on guidance to obtain some desired object. Words and sentences are not used for the purpose of engaging in social interaction.

Scott's inventory of language is not sufficiently well developed to support the kind of repeated questioning or statements about some topic that are seen in Level 5.0. Scott may respond to a statement or question with a movement or an action, but almost never replies with a spoken statement.

Domain 3. Types of Interests.

The participant's behavior is so self-isolating that it is extremely difficult to understand what his interests are, other than repeated body movements or sensory stimulation, as with patterns of lights, the sounds of his voice, or the texture of his clothing.

He will typically focus his attention on a narrow segment of a larger event, such as throwing a ball rather than playing a game of baseball, or moving a single checker on a board instead of playing a full game of checkers.

The participants at this Level have no interest in responding to an audience, and are unconcerned about the ways in which an audience might react to them.

Domain 4. Personal Management and Self-Direction.

At this Level the participant does not have the personal management functions that are needed to structure, define, and coordinate his daily activities. Scott definitely requires the input of another person to provide structuring, guidance, oversight and corrective interventions. Given careful, skilled and ongoing teaching the participant and his Same-Level peers can learn to use a variety of cues and prompts (such as signs, icons, simple pictures, etc.) to travel through the day's schedule of activities. The overall framework of that schedule needs to be designed, adjusted, and sustained by someone else.

In the absence of these structures and supports the participant would slide into a state of self-preoccupation and disorganization.

Domain 5. Language Understanding. Receptive Language.

For this participant there is almost no observable development of word-understanding or of meaningful reactions to other people's spoken language. Scott offers almost no attention to other people's statements or questions. Scott and the Same-Level participants show no understanding of complicated sentences and no understanding of figures of speech or idioms.

The participant offers no reactions or replies to statements made to him by unfamiliar people. In such circumstances there are no practical differences between what is not known versus what is totally ignored. Scott also does not reply or appropriately react to newly-introduced or spontaneous speech. The statements or phrases to which he might respond are those which have been previously well-practiced and rehearsed.

As with participants at the previous Levels, a hearing loss was suspected before the age of three. In most cases that question was put aside after an examination.

Because the participant often does not act in response to spoken words and short-sentence requests alone, the speaker may need to use hands-on guidance and prompts, such as demonstrations and modeling, in order to have the action successfully completed. The speaker may also use American Sign Language and picture boards.

Scott and other participants at this Level offer only a very limited range of cooperation or appropriate reactions to a very small number of very familiar trusted people, usually no more than two or three.

Domain 6. Social Use of Language. Pragmatic Language.

The communications produced by this participant are very limited, and may seem more like a pre-language style than one of standard language. Scott is unaware of the subtle nuances of language – neither his own nor those of others.

He does not want to interact with others, and has considerable difficulty communicating with spoken language about his basic needs or wants. It is very difficult for other people to know, at a given moment, what this participant needs. The parents, caregivers, or teachers understand that they need to rely on "reading" Scott's spontaneous body language, expressions and vocalizations.

Domain 7. Body Language. Nonverbal Communication.

(The previously stated qualifiers apply to this Domain.) Scott does not notice body language, facial expressions and gestures of other people. He does not intentionally use body language, facial expressions and gestures to communicate his own ideas, intentions and needs.

Scott does not engage in conversation and does not attend to the speaker. He works energetically to avoid personal interactions and eye contact. Scott avoids interaction or withdraws when other people get close to entering his personal space. If withdrawing from interaction is inconvenient he might aggressively push away other people.

Domain 8. Flexibility and Transitions.

Scott is extremely immersed and focused on his routines, procedures, behavior rituals and personal interests. These routines and personal interests are the ruling realities of his life. They push aside just about every other activity or possible experience. He has no interests in exploring other activities, places, events or skills. A very narrow range of repeated activity occupies his waking hours.

Scott firmly and energetically resists changes to his self-selected routines. His resistance can be silently unmoving or actively angry and protesting, even to the point of becoming aggressive.

Any attempt to introduce slight changes in activities, new people, or small changes in his routine must be done very thoughtfully, slowly, and with great skill over an extended span of time.

Domain 9. Repeating Body Movements. Movement Stereotypes.

(The previously mentioned qualifiers apply to this Domain.) Scott produces 3 or more types of the unusual repeating movements, listed below, as often as 16 to 36 times per day. On some days they

may be even more frequent. These incidents are wide-spread and ongoing.

1. Walking on tiptoes.
2. Whirling or turning in a circle.
3. Flapping of the hands.
4. Rocking back-and-forth, either while sitting or standing.
5. Wiggling or flicking the fingers.
6. Slapping the side of the body.

Scott's repeating movements and self-hurting behaviors are nearly constant, and tend to dominate his activities and schedule. The frequency and intensity of these behaviors make it very difficult to engage him in useful or productive activities. The conditions for achieving school-based learning are very challenging.

The nature of Scott's self-hurting behaviors can make it necessary to use protective clothing and accessories, such as gloves and protective headgear.

Domain 10. Creative Imagination.

Scott shows many of the same behaviors as someone who is at Level 6.0, but his overall range of functioning is even more limited. Rather than playing with objects as symbols, models or imaginative characters he uses them in a highly ritualized and unusual way. For instance, he may rub the soft covering of a teddy bear against his cheek, over and over, but not imaginatively pretend that the teddy bear can role play.

Scott never developed imaginative play nor did he produce make-believe stories, either independently or in cooperation with someone else. His daily activities are mostly determined by what is immediately in front of him. He does not use imagination as a resource and does not engage in creative thinking or constructive problem-solving. He does not engage in shared fantasies or imaginative stories with anyone.

He might be able to understand the concept of "tomorrow". However, he is likely to need additional explanation in order to understand time concepts that go much beyond "tomorrow".

Domain 11. Imitation & Empathy.

The ability of Scott to imitate and copy behavior is present to only the smallest extent. He is able to move through his daily schedule only with the application of ongoing, steady guidance, support and coaching.

He learns the general outline of the day's activities and can retain this learning for a brief time, perhaps a few days or weeks. However, unless the guidance, support and coaching are continued regularly the learning will be lost and he will slide into a completely non-interactive, self-occupied condition.

Scott is unable to imitate spoken sounds and the words that are built from those sounds. As a result, he has no clearly spoken language. He focuses his attention on his own thoughts, feelings, sensations, movements and needs. It is only with direct, close face-to-face communication and hands-on guidance and directions that he will briefly focus on another person or re-direct his attention.

When left to his own preferences he has no awareness of and no interest in another person's experiences, wishes, moods or plans.

Domain 12. Unusual Sensory Events.

All of the sensory fascinations and rejections that are described in Levels 5.0 and 6.0 are also seen at this Level (7.0) with this participant. There can be 20 or more episodes a day for any of these behaviors.

The intense fascination and aggressive avoidance Scott shows for certain sensory stimuli pose very large and persistent obstacles for him. These extreme reactions work against the formation of pleasant social relationships, the acquisition of skill and knowledge through education and meaningful participation in his community.

Epilogue

There dwell among us those who travel the path more slowly, who find fascination in scenes we rarely see, whose preference is to heed their own counsel. The measure of our community can be taken from the ways in which we comfort, shelter and school those special travelers. Their contribution to the global village are those lessons we have managed to learn about growing toward a more generous, wiser and more caring human family. Let them be seen, let them be heard, and let them be embraced.

Sidney Ganzler © 2017

Selected References For
On The Level

American Psychiatric Association: Diagnostic and Statistical Manual of Mental Disorders, Fourth Edition, Text Revision. Washington, DC, American Psychiatric Association, 2006

American Psychiatric Association, Diagnostic and Statistical Manual of Mental Disorders, Fifth Edition. Washington, DC, American Psychiatric Association, 2013.

Baron-Cohen, S. (1988). Social and pragmatic deficits in autism. Cognitive or affective? Journal of Autism and Developmental Disorders, 18 (3), 379-402.

Bauer, S. (1996). Asperger Syndrome. *The O.A.S.I.S. (Online Asperger Syndrome Information and Support* [TM]*) Web Page.* Retrieved January 9, 1998 from http://www.udeledu/bkirby/asperger/as thru years.html

Brinton, Bonnie. (1984), Elementary school age children's comprehension of specific idiomatic expressions. *Journal of Communication Disorders,* 18 (4), 245-257.

Ganzler, S. and Sherman, K. (2011). The Continuum Of Autism Spectrum Traits, COAST. Currently

undergoing validity research. Unpublished
Text.

Gibbs, Raymond, J. (1991). Semantic analyzability
in children's understanding of idioms. *Journal
of Speech and Hearing Research,* 34, 613-629,

Klin, A. and Volkmar, F.R. (1995) Asperger
syndrome: Some guidelines for assessment,
diagnosis, and intervention. *Learning
Disabilities Association of America.* Retrieved
January 9, 1998, from
http://info.med.yaleedu/childstdy/autism/Asper
ger-dxhtml

Pexman.M.G. (2009) Development of children's
ability to distinguish sarcasm and verbal irony.
Journal of Child Language. 37 (02), 429-451